AF473706

lucio fontana

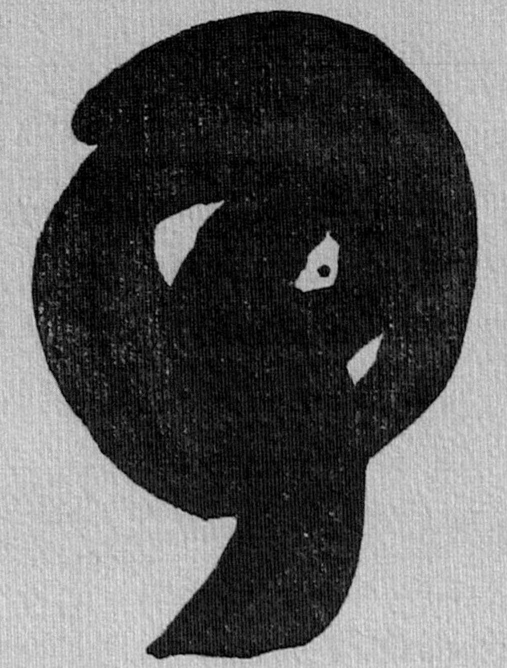

GOOD MORNING TO FONTANA

Good morn, morning to you
Milanese from Santa Fé
Pioneering Milanese
Of planets in the make:
Three generations'
Scandal and pride!
Most precious prick
And warp and drill
To our miserable space
Of mice in the cheese
Tinned sardines
Filled with mythology
& the classical school.

Good morn, morning to you
The astral's worker
Turner of black eggs
Spheres' contractor
Other day's
Worlds and globes!
As sharp as a diamond
Always on the lookout
Where earth
And sky clash
Space's fruitful
Slasher and fugleman
Of the great cosmic zero.

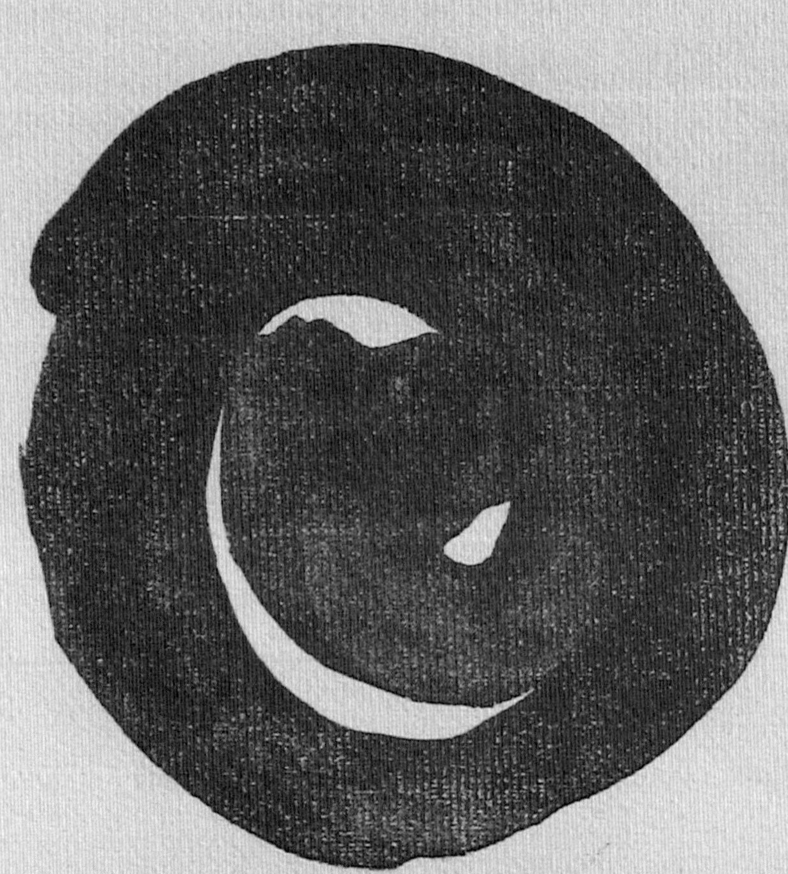

(trad. di Mary de Rachewiltz)

lucio fontana

WORKS FROM 1936 TO 1965

text by
Paolo Campiglio

AMEDEO PORRO FINE ARTS
BEN BROWN FINE ARTS

SilvanaEditoriale

Cover
Concetto spaziale, 1955
Ballerina, 1952

Page 2
Good Morning to Fontana by Raffaele Carrieri, with drawings by Lucio Fontana, central page of the exhibition catalogue Fontana - New York, Galleria dell'Ariete, June 1962

Project and realization
Amedeo Porro Fine Arts, Lugano
Ben Brown Fine Arts, London

Catalogue
Paolo Campiglio

Historical scientific sheets and notes
Paolo Campiglio

Archive sources
Archivio della Fondazione Lucio Fontana, Milan

All works are registered in the archive of the Fondazione Lucio Fontana, Milan

Amedeo Porro and Ben Brown are extremely grateful to the Fondazione Lucio Fontana for their courteous, constant and invaluable co-operation.

Many thanks to
Enrico Crispolti, Rome
Giulio Tega and Vita Stolova, Lugano;
Massimo Di Carlo, Galleria Dello Scudo, Verona;
Marco Voena and Edmondo di Robilant, London

Photographic credits
Archivio Giancolombo
Paolo Vandrasch
Domus

Restorer
Francesco Mesiti, Turin
Barbara Ferriani, Milan

Amedeo Porro Fine Arts
Federica Boragina

Ben Brown Fine Arts
Christopher Baer
Jemma Beeley
Silvia Davoli
Emilie Ortolan
Stefanie Roggensack

Amedeo Porro Fine Arts SA
Via Motta 17
6900 Lugano, Switzerland
t. +41 79 699 61 75
gallery@amedeoporrofinearts.com
www.amedeoporrofinearts.com

Ben Brown Fine Arts
12 Brook's Mews
London W1K4DG, United Kingdom
t. +44 20 7734 8888
f. +44 20 7734 8892
info@benbrownfinearts.com
www.benbrownfinearts.com

I am very proud to present, alongside my good friend Amedeo Porro, this catalogue of works by Lucio Fontana, one of the greatest Italian artists of the 20th Century. Herein, you will find an impressive selection of iconic *tagli, buchi* and *pietre* paintings as well as ceramics and sculptures spanning the breadth of Fontana's career as an artist.

As a dealer, collector and champion of 20th Century Italian art, I feel that Fontana's ceramics are underappreciated and undervalued, an inequality I am determined to resolve. The ceramics are a less well known facet of Fontana's oeuvre but a medium he continued to explore from his early days right through to the end of his life.

Included in our catalogue is *Concetto Spaziale* (1962), the only ceramic which was exhibited in the acclaimed 1977 Guggenheim retrospective.

The Lucio Fontana exhibition at the Hayward Gallery in 1999 went some way to rectifying this underrepresentation as have other recent museum shows including the beautiful exhibition at the Musée d'Art Moderne de La Ville de Paris in 2014.

This project is the result of many years' work and it has been a pleasure to collaborate with Amedeo Porro, whose in-depth knowledge of Fontana's work and close relationship with the Fondazione Fontana has been an invaluable help. I also want to thank Paolo Campiglio, whose insightful text and comprehensive understanding of Fontana's work has been vital.

For the experienced collector and novice alike, I hope that this catalogue will inspire an interest in and love for the work of Lucio Fontana.

BEN BROWN

Contents

"...I would like to participate in the Venice Biennale with the Ambiente Spaziale..."

PAOLO CAMPIGLIO

Since his debut, in the second half of the 1920s, Fontana's choice to prefer research art implied his aware opposition to the surrounding – and often narrow – provincial environments, and his openness to a wider scene, a long-distance exchange with internationally renowned artists. In Argentina, in the small town of Rosario, information on European research was hard to obtain, but in 1925 his friend, painter Julio Vanzo – with whom Fontana shared a studio in calle Rioja 2070 for some time – motivated him to look at the results of Esprit Nouveau, at the solutions of Léger and Le Corbusier, to study Archipenko's 'sculpto-paintings', although only at a visual level, frantically leafing through magazines. Fontana trained in Milan and considered himself to be half European, besides Argentine, he loved Futurism, knew the work of Boccioni as a sculptor, which he would appreciate for his entire life and which would be at the origin of Spatialism; he had a passion for Van Gogh and Matisse, and maybe even saw some of the smaller sculptures of the latter, but he was seduced by Archipenko, an Ukrainian sculptor recently migrated to the United States. His first research works, such as *Nudo* (Nude,1926), in gilded plaster, *Mujer y el balde* (1926), *Ballerina di Charleston* (Charleston dancer,1926), displayed in the exhibition of the Nexus group in Rosario – an avant-garde group of young artists, up-to-date on European and American art – reveal his reasoning on post-cubist sculpture.

It was the beginning of a path of expressive freedom, coming at a high cost, which would expose him to criticism and incomprehension by his contemporaries, for the sake of a higher concept of art and of those beliefs that would be his only reasons for living.

A further step occurred in the 1930s, when he moved to Italy for the first time; Italy was the place where he developed and expressed his unusual sculptural concepts, which the public and critics were unable to understand and only had a few admirers. Among them, Edoardo Persico and young architects such as Luigi Figini and Gino Pollini, Ernesto Rogers, among others, and the BBPR group, looking at the European scene of Mies Van der Rohe and Le Corbusier. In Milan, the theories of Zadkine, Brancusi, the 'vitalist' sculpture of an artist without a homeland such as Ernesto De Fiori seduced young Fontana during his research. His first painted sculptures, the *Uomo nero* (Black man,1930), the constructivist design for the monument to Grandi (1931), the *tavolette graffite* (scratched panels) of 1931, the abstract sculptures of 1934 and his very participation, together with Fausto Melotti, in Abstraction-Création in 1935 already suggested that the young artist had chosen an international dimension as his space for debate, rather than Italy only, which at the time was unfortunately entrenched in a nationalist perspective. His coloured plaster and clay works and his abstract sculptures represent his first open exchange with a European context, an always vigilant and critical debate expressing his alternative ideas, rather than an actual reliance on one style or another. A restless and free vitalism leads him through his fluctuations between representation and abstraction, in the belief that the sculptural fact speaks as an emanation of his own human nature: it is the reality of the work – not only the theoretical reasons underlying it – that determines the artistic fact. And Fontana is looking for something else, he is not satisfied with the ambiguity of a certain geometric Abstract Art, he loves Surrealism's automatic drawing and graffiti, but he is not so keen on its – often abused – iconography of the unconscious and cannot accept the social revolution endorsed by Breton: he wants to go beyond volume, bypass separations between sculpture and painting, but in doing so he follows a winding path, leading him to contradict Brancusi too. And colour – which, according to Fontana, represents the light that nullifies volume – acquires a crucial value within this liberation of shape: red, pink, light blue, violet and pistachio green, black and white, gold and silver are the tones used by the artist over that decade to paint the surface of his sculptural works and abstract structures. Totally artificial colours, never seen in the nature, which could maybe be found in some of those Kandinsky's watercolours displayed at the Milione Gallery in 1934: rationalist and modern tones, with a touch of sensuality and baroque taste.

The experience with ceramic sculpture, which began in Albisola in 1936 and continued during Autumn 1937 in the Manufacture de Sèvres, should be seen as a further, extraordinary liberation of shape and, at the same time, as a first instance of international debate on polychrome sculpture, in the framework of a neo-naturalist morphology: Fontana intended to promote his idea of coloured ceramic sculpture in France, and even thought of moving to Paris on a permanent basis, at the same time as his majolica works displayed at the Ceramic pavilion (with Manifattura Mazzotti) in the Exposition Internationale des Arts et des techniques dans la vie moderne were being awarded prizes. During his first stay in Paris, between Summer and late November 1937, Fontana came into contact with Tristan Tzara and discussed the meaning of volume with Brancusi: while they insisted on the overcoming of 'volume' in sculptural works, Fontana put forward the concept of 'space', already introduced by Boccioni.[1] This anecdote is mentioned in Fontana's conversation with Carla Lonzi in 1967: "Back in 1931-1932, I was already looking for thread sculpture ('*scultura a fili*'), rather than volume ... I had discussed with Brancusi and Tristan Tzara ... I deeply admire Brancusi, but he is always shape, and I told him that those were amazing things within a period, but that Boccioni was already there with his *Muscoli in movimento* (*Forze uniche nella continuità dello spazio*), which I thought it was a more important discovery than his, because, while he valued matter both in a sculptural and spatial way, matter was a secondary issue to Boccioni, light entered matter, hence marble was no longer a concern."[2] However, following the two exhibitions in Paris, at the gallery of Madame Jeanne Bucher and at Galerie Zack, the young artist was forced to pack his bags and go back to Milan: the time was not yet ripe for him to move to Paris for good, even though his works did arouse some admiration. When Carola Gedion-Welcker included his works in the volume *Moderne Plastik: Elemente der Wirklichkeit, Masse und Auflockerung* (1937), it seemed like the beginning of an international attention towards his work, but that was just an illusion, as the following years spent in Argentina (1940–47) and most of all the Second World War would nullify Fontana's work and call for a new start. As a matter of fact, the Argentine artistic environment was still not receptive enough, with the exception of the young artists that followed Fontana after 1945; and nevertheless, the artist exploited this sort of separation from the European world as a reason for re-launching and re-working his theories.

The artist's return to Milan, in April 1947, in the light of the premises developed in Buenos Aires in 1946, was a double challenge: with himself, and his ideal

belief in the rejuvenation of art's traditional shapes and means, regardless of the issues of painting and sculpture, beyond abstraction and representation.
In any case, it is interesting to point out that, within this new path, the artist never saw ceramic as an inheritance from the past, but rather as a constant reason for change, in the same way as his first *Concetti spaziali* (Spatial concepts) developed in 1947. In 1948, Lisa Ponti, keeping in mind the artist's past experiences of cooperation with architects, wrote as follows in *Domus*, in the framework of her review of an exhibition of Fontana's ceramics:

> Today, Fontana becomes spatial: we shall explain you this movement, arisen in 1946 in Buenos Aires and in May 1947 in Milan, with a declamatory manifesto written by intellectuals, and whose members met and discussed in the studios of architects Belgioioso and Rogers, at the Naviglio and at Sassu's: what seems reliable to us is the presence of Fontana, of his good faith and undeniable happy nature [...] As the most exciting adventures, visions and discoveries of treasures occur to ordinary people, who can tell them in a few words, in the same way Fontana sails by foot on the secret sea of 'spatial sculpture': he must find, he says, a new way of sculpture which, just like television, takes advantage of space, motion and lights, now that all the old ways are exhausted, to give new life to art.[3]

This challenge, through the manifestos of Spatialism and the gathering of a group of young members of the new movement, was launched, first and foremost, on a national level and especially in Milan, among architects and the few admirers Carlo Cardazzo and Milena Milani, Beniamino Joppolo. In spite of this, as usual, the artist aimed at achieving a perspective of reasoning that was more open to debate among disciplines, in a supranational dimension: this is evidenced by his participation in the Venice Biennale in the 1950s, which gives a fair representation of his underlying contradiction between the struggle for success as a key player of modernity, the desire to be known by his most experimental and radically 'spatialist' works and the narrowness of the Italian cultural background, with which his proposals were doomed

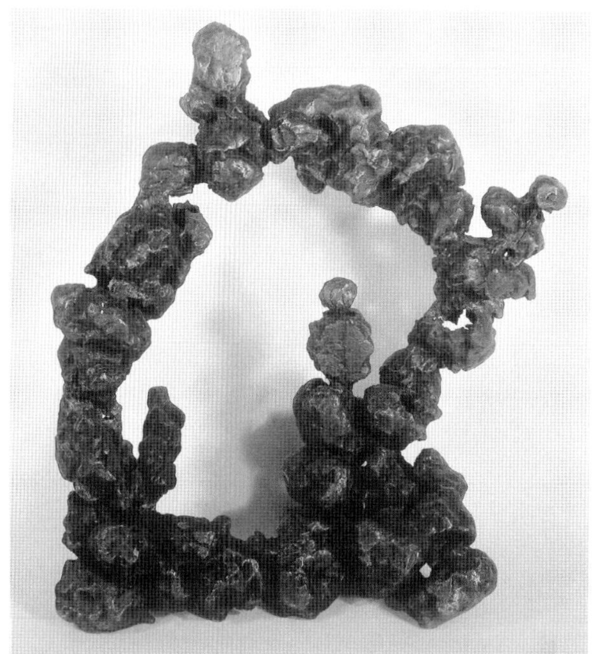

Scultura spaziale, 1947

to clash, and, as a corollary, the incomprehension of contemporary international critics.
Fontana had already displayed his works at the Venice Biennale back in 1930, but that had been a first chance of notoriety promoted by his old master Wildt, who was in the committee, followed by a silence that had lasted for 18 years.
In the first post-war international event, at the XXIV Venice Biennale in 1948, the artist presented five works: three ceramics, the large mosaic *Gallo* (Rooster, 1948) – later purchased by the Rome National Gallery – and above all the *Scultura spaziale* (Spatial sculpture, 1947). Works made of ceramic and mosaic together with spatial works, reasserting the compatibility of Fontana's branches of research. In this anti-sculpture (the corollary of which was the *Concetto spaziale* (Spatial concept, 1947), sort of mutilated, oppressive human figure, a metaphor for men in the atomic age, the artist deals with the problem of representing space through a matter that draws a circular crown, a ring, leaving an empty space that becomes the key element at the core of the composition: it is a return to the roots, to the first man on earth, with

an image that can either lead back to the beginning of the world or suggest a future in the space, the slow rarefaction of galactic matter or a bright atomic mushroom. This notwithstanding, the work went unnoticed at the international exhibition and no reaction came from the critics attending the Venice Biennale.
The 'spatial' nuclear analysis resumed in 1948 and 1949, in some gouaches used as preparation material for the *Ambiente spaziale* (Spatial environment, 1949) at the Naviglio Gallery in Milan, and in a group of ceramics where the spiral becomes a metaphor for a material vortex, for a concentration of the mass.[4] Whilst, due to its amazing originality, the *Ambiente spaziale* (1949) triggered the Italian press reaction, though for a short period of five days only, and achieved the expected goal to promote the first public performance of the Spatial Movement, the only world-renowned magazine that, in May of the same year, put a nice colour reproduction of Fontana's invention on its cover was *Domus*, edited by Gio Ponti.
Thus, it is no surprise that the artist's goal was to present the *Ambiente spaziale* again at the XXV Venice Biennale in 1950 (or to create a new one), where he was invited, in order to give a sharper and more spectacular message. Namely, on 19th November 1949, from Albisola, Fontana wrote to Rodolfo Pallucchini as follows:[5]

> Dear Sir /I would like to participate in the Venice Biennale with the "Ambiente Spaziale"; I therefore kindly ask you to inform the members of the Invitation Committee about this request of mine. Should you or the Committee deem it appropriate, I can send you in a more [deleted] detailed fashion what my intentions and reasons are in relation to the Spatial controversy. /Waiting for your kind reply, I send my best regards/Lucio Fontana/Via Piccinni 1/Milan/N.B. Albissola Capo/Ristorante Pescetto/Savona

On 26th November 1949, Pallucchini sent his reply to Fontana, addressed to the Pescetto restaurant in Albisola Capo:[6]

> Dear Sir, /If only I had received your letter dated 19th November a few days earlier, I would have certainly informed the Committee, and perhaps I would have asked you to send me some other explanatory materials on the spatial environment and controversy, to be added to what is already present in our Historical Archive of Contemporary Art; unfortunately, the Committee met on 12th and 13th, that is to say many days before you wrote to me. / In those sessions, the Committee defined the plan for the Exhibition and drew up the proposals to be submitted to the Chairman as for invitations. Although – for obvious reasons – I am not in the position to discuss with you in details any decision made as far as you are concerned, I believe you shall not be displeased with what you are shortly to be officially notified. /Kind regards.

Since the chance to create an *ambiente* (environment) had faded, at the Biennale in 1950 the artist displayed his ceramic sculptures again, a production upon which his scarce international visibility relied at that time. On the other hand, the artist made his visibility much more explicit with his second environmental work, having the nature of a programme, after the *Ambiente spaziale*: the *Concetto spaziale* at the IX Milan Triennale (1951), a seamless line of neon lights that unfolds – at a remarkable height – against the light-blue ceiling of the Milan Triennale designed by architects Baldessari and Grisotti. At that time, the work was actually reproduced by international architecture magazines such as Interiors, New York, and Fontana was one of the lecturers of the International Congress on Proportions (1951), where he presented his *Manifesto tecnico* alongside Le Corbusier, Max Bill, Vantongerloo to endorse the reasons of his art.
Building on the success of the *Concetto spaziale* at the IX Milan Triennale, on 14th September 1951 Fontana made a second attempt to bring forth an *Ambiente spaziale* in the framework of the XXVI Venice Biennale in 1952, as we can read in a new letter sent to Pallucchini:[7]

> Milan, 14th September 1951 / Prof. Rodolfo Pallucchini / Venice Biennale Secretary General / Dear Professor, / I am sending this to you as I would like you to endorse my request before the Invitation Committee for the next Biennale, thus obtaining a small space to arrange the "Ambiente Spaziale", which was not possible during the latest Biennale, since my request had come too late. / I would

> keep available, in case they ask for them, papers, controversies and works (pictures) by the spatialists. / I also allow myself to inform you that, in France, a movement has recently been founded by architects and artists, called 'Groupe Espace', whose concepts are the same as those stated in the Italian Group's manifestos of 1947 and 1948. I therefore now hope that my request is not included in some imaginary order and is kept into account. / Thank you and regards. / Lucio Fontana / Via Prina 7

At first, Pallucchini's reply sent to Fontana, at via Prina 7 in Milan, on 17th September 1951, sounded positive:[8]

> Venice, 17 September 1951/ Dear Mr Fontana, I received your letter dated 14th September and I would like to assure you that I took note of the contents you expressed therein, and that I shall not fail to inform the Committee in charge of arranging the exhibition about them / Kind regards.

But following Alberto Magnelli's decision not to take on that role, Pallucchini suggested appointing Fontana as a member of the XXVI Biennale Executive Committee, and the latter accepted to participate also with a view to promoting the Spatialist group. The committee was chaired by Roberto Longhi, with the involvement of Pallucchini, and was made up by Pericle Fazzini and Carlo Alberto Petrucci, members of the International Expert Board, among which Luigi Montanarini – then representative of the National Federation of Figurative Art Independent Trade Unions, and Publio Morbiducci – representative of the CISL, Paolo Ricci – representative of the CGIL, and artists Enrico Paolucci, Enrico Prampolini, Giuseppe Santomaso. In the meetings held in Venice, one of the first decisions voted by the Committee – with the opposition of Fontana and Santomaso – was the exclusion of the artist members of the Committee itself from the exhibition: thus, the project of a new *Ambiente spaziale* immediately faded. Furthermore, since the very first meeting, Fontana and Fazzini proposed a retrospective on Balla, strongly opposed by the other members of the Committee, and disapproved the participation of Sironi, Casorati, Rosai: from the minutes, it actually emerges that the artist "claimed that ten years ago these 'elderly men' had had their own exhibition rooms at the Biennale and now it would be fair to leave those exhibition rooms to the youngsters." As far as solo exhibition rooms to youngsters were concerned, the trend endorsed by Santomaso, among others, was the one of the 'abstract-concrete' group, which would be presented by Lionello Venturi, and whose members included Afro, Birolli, Cassinari, Morlotti, among others; but Fontana did not consider Vedova as good as Birolli and Cassinari, while supporting Aligi Sassu and, among sculptors, Agenore Fabbri. During the following meeting, with a view to broadening participation to the so-called 'very youngsters', Fontana "raised the issue of 'spatialists'" and "upon request of some of the members of the Committee, explained these new trends of spatial and nuclear artists and mentioned, for Milan, Dova, Peverelli, Crippa, Dangelo, Baj, Dorazio, Carozzi and Joppolo." At a later stage, Fontana "engaged in a long battle for long-time abstract artists from Milan, especially in relation to those from Rome",[9] but his proposal was rejected by the majority. He was only allowed to replace Lilloni with Spilimbergo. Out of the group of spatialists, only Crippa and Dova would display their works, while Peverelli, invited for graphics, would decline.

By the next Biennale, the XXVII edition (1954), where he was invited as a sculptor with his own solo room, Fontana was no longer thinking about the *Ambiente spaziale,* and for the first time he imagined his own retrospective exhibition, with a set-up of green walls and black bases for sculptures: the important thing to be considered is that, in the context of this first historical vision of his work, he insisted on establishing a relationship between his pre-spatial research of 1931 *tavolette graffite* or 1934 abstract sculptures and his latest, 1952 spatial production, and namely spatial concepts with holes, highlighting the continuity of his research from the 1930s to the 1950s. Ultimately, 18 works were displayed in the room, which in 1957 was still referred to by critic Valsecchi as a scandal, both because the artist contradicted the traditional separation between sculpture and painting, and because his spatial concepts with holes on paper, paperboard or canvas could not be pigeonholed – neither in geometric abstraction, nor in figurative realism – and were incomprehensible to most people, in spite of the introduction to the exhibition catalogue by Giampiero Giani. This is so true, that, as evidenced by the correspondence with Pallucchini, spatial paintings were "rudely beaten" by the public, the holes were "torn and altered" for the whole duration of the exhibition, which resulted in the artist's deep resentment. This notwithstanding, and in spite of the controversy aroused, the exhibition room still had no effect on the international press.[10]

To a certain extent, 1954 historical experience was the prelude to the wider invitation received for the XXIX Biennale in 1958, where Fontana arranged a remarkable solo exhibition room which – finally – attracted an unprecedented interest from the French culture, and even from the Anglo-Saxon world. The new circle, which opened especially towards London, would prove itself to be of crucial relevance for Lucio, and was essentially the result of the efforts and friendship of a prominent collector, patron and manager: Italian-Argentine Carlo Damiano, then executive of Pirelli House in London. This international turning point took place at the same time as the 1958 Biennale, which therefore represented a key moment for the diffusion of a certain image of the artist abroad.

Indeed, between 1954 and 1957, Fontana, besides having 'translated' the issue of the *Ambiente spaziale* into a number of spectacular collaborations with architecture – in the Milan Fiera, in the Triennale and in private commissions – especially in the framework of spatial ceilings, variedly changed his imagination in connection with works on canvas: first and foremost, with his increasingly more elaborate *pietre* (stones), with pieces of Murano glass applied on punctured canvas, he introduced a further dimension of bright or translucent matter, in dialogue with the timeless reference of the hole, aimed at the infinite; in addition to that, he started the more complex series of the *barocchi* (baroques), reconfirming his sparkling material imagination while, at the same time, relaxing – within a fruitful debate between matter and antimatter – in the *gessi* (impastos) series, showing harmonious curved shapes obtained by using impastos of pastel paints, scraps of canvas on canvas and a lowered material texture; finally, he developed the *inchiostri* (inks), even lighter paintings coloured with anilines, with new shapes of canvas cut out as collages, where a taste inspired by 'emptiness' and antimatter is evident instead; as evidenced, these are 'cloud-like' canvases, expressing a feeling of calm which also emerges from contemporary 'stalk' sculptures (1957–58), plant-like works reproducing the same shapes and translating them into sculpture.

Both these series show a return to the medium of pure canvas, within a perspective of a sharper laydown of colour, while at the same time an imagination of whole and complete 'shapes' re-emerges, showing metaphorical – rather than naturalistic – features. The image of shape has always been in his mind, since his first plaster *tavolette graffite* at the beginning of the 1930s, and the artist would seem to resort to arched silhouettes and colour – a colour that is more pictorial here than anywhere else – almost as if he missed a 'tabula rasa' or a 'formal', and therefore 'formative', alternative layout for the work, which is a feature that is always present in his imagination. Some of these formal works – showing a transverse development and thinning down into stems, or stalks, that call to mind seaweeds or plants – have been studied by the artist for a long time in a number of sketches, and then presented again in the contemporary iron sculpture.

From 4th June to 31st July 1957, prior to the setting up of the room at the Biennale and thanks to the commitment, as a manager, of his friend Damiano, among the trustees of the Tate Gallery – who had been in contact with Lawrence Alloway, then assistant director of the Institute of Contemporary Art (I.C.A.) and with Herbert Read, director of the I.C.A., since late 1957 – Fontana managed to display some of his works with Crippa and Dova at the exhibition *Between space and earth. Trends in Italian Art*, organised on the initiative of Eric Estorick and Damiano at the Marlborough Gallery in London, with the explicit aim to spread the spatial movement in London. The exhibition was introduced by Alloway, who was the first to write about Fontana's works in the United Kingdom.[11]

The room at the 1958 Biennale was set up by Carlo Scarpa and today it is also well-known thanks to

Fontana's Hall at Venice Biennale, 1958
(photo Giancolombo)

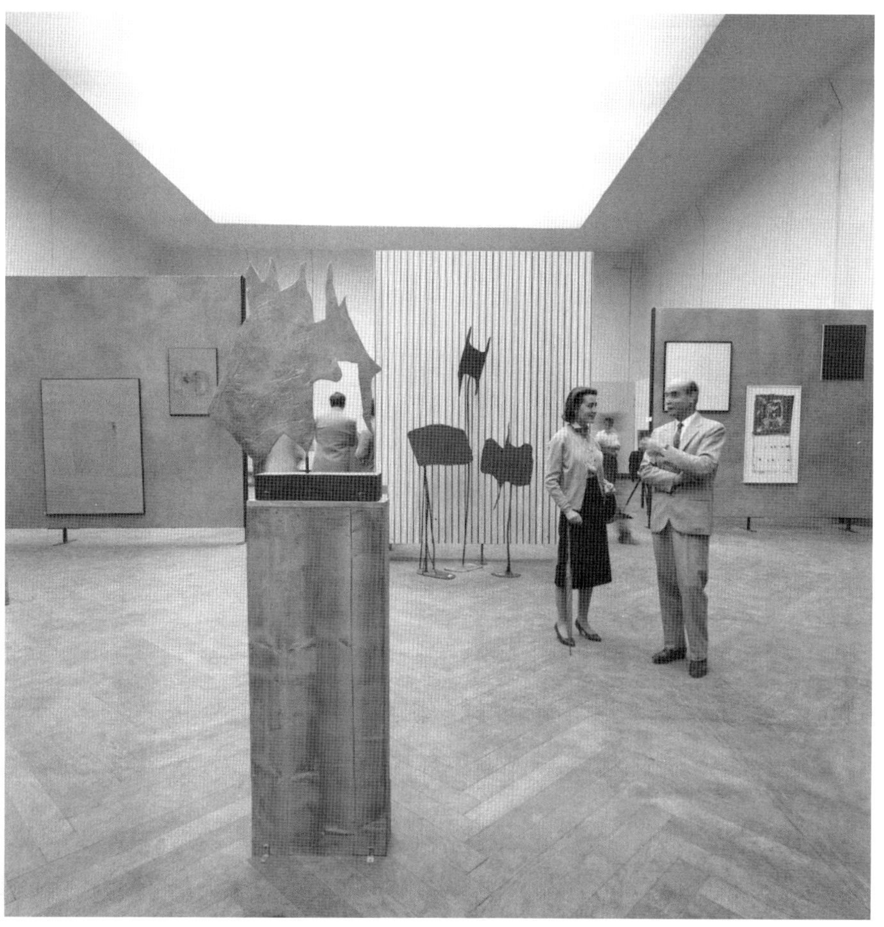

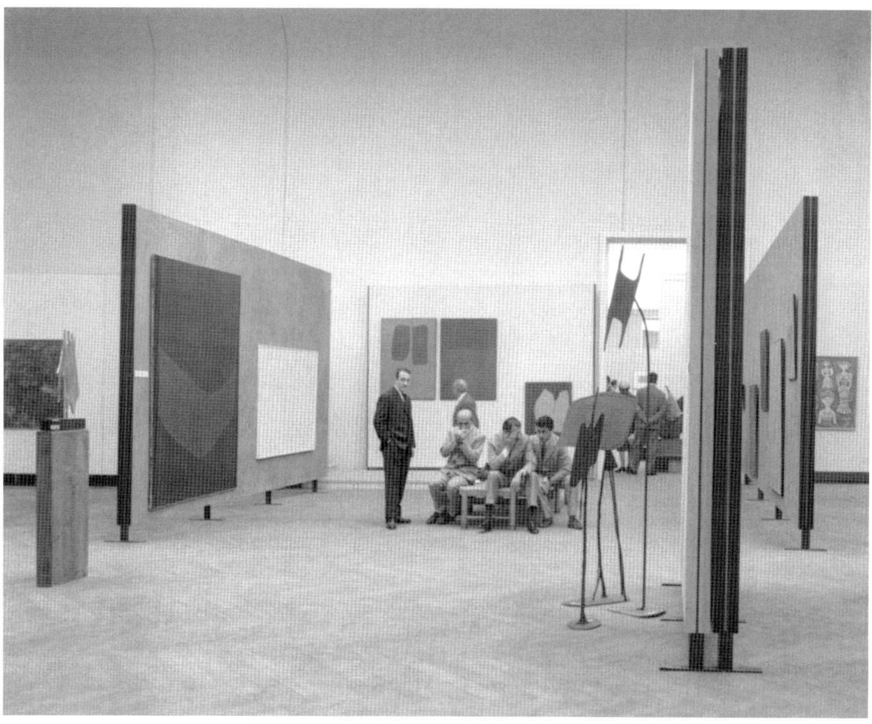

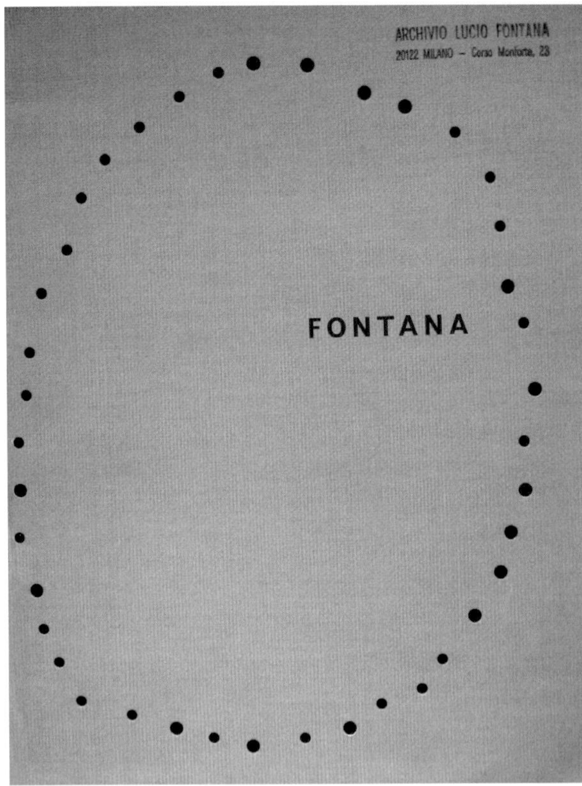

Ten painting of Venice, Martha Jackson Gallery, 21 November - 16 December 1961

a photo shoot by photographer Giancolombo and to the pictures taken for a piece published by Elle; just like in 1954, though in a more paradigmatic way, the room renewed the bond between the issue of 'shape' and the experiences of the 1930s: once again, Fontana displayed two original *tavolette graffite*, two reworked abstract sculptures from 1934, a few *barocchi*, among which the renowned *Gogotha* of Antonio Boschi, and several new works, most of all *gessi* and *inchiostri*,[12] some of which of remarkable size. The room is magically suspended in a metaphysical aura, where the common thread between old and new works creates an impression of a real 'environment', thus shocking even the most influential critics and impressing young Enrico Crispolti: namely, it pushed him to perform a diachronic analysis of the artist's work, beyond preconceptions and beyond the usual judgement of the 'expedient'. In the introduction to the exhibition catalogue, by Guido Ballo, the author mentioned the "essentiality of pure origins", the "evocation of undefined spaces", and so the artist, following that relevant, first international success, turned his work again towards a new, increasingly more radical essentiality, which went through the experience of the *carte* (papers), already cut and torn by lacerations, and thanks to that beginning, in late 1958, came to the *tagli* (slashes).

In particular, the outrage of the *carte* – of which the *Concetto spaziale* (1958) represents an emblematic solution – seems to bring the artist back to the essentiality of his first, large punctured papers of 1949: there, the galactic rarefaction of holes expressed a drastic solution, whereby colour was given up, that could be initially enhanced by backlighting. Indeed, back then the critics had talked about "screens". On the other hand, in the papers on canvas of 1958, slightly earlier and contemporary with the *tagli*, the artist evidenced the pure sequentiality of an essential gesture within the raw space of the work. And the gesture is the hand moving through the space, scratching the white surface of paper and straining against it until it breaks. A simple and elementary process that is, a new coded sequence in which the artist takes up the challenge together with the style he uses. In this sense, the *carte* anticipate the *tagli* on monochrome canvas and are their prerequisite.

Meanwhile, in 1958, Fontana's work found an explanation and a unique interpretation in the Anglo-Saxon world, mediated by the critical production of Alloway, as recently evidenced by Francesco Tedeschi:[13] those of his 1957–58 works that are more related to the concept of 'shape' were construed by Alloway as having a new 'figurative' meaning, not in its narrative sense, but rather as an unconscious expression of new formal structures to be found in the mass imagination; which was different from the then-known contemporary informal interpretation developed by Greenberg. In the introduction to the exhibition *Paintings from Damiano Collection* – meanwhile organised by the manager at the ICA in London (7th January - 7th February 1959), just after having purchased some of the artist's *gessi* and at least one *taglio* – Alloway construed the 'holes' that he saw in the *gessi* as signifying signs, rather than obscure lacerations: "Holes in pictures are usually a sign of ruin, but the patterns

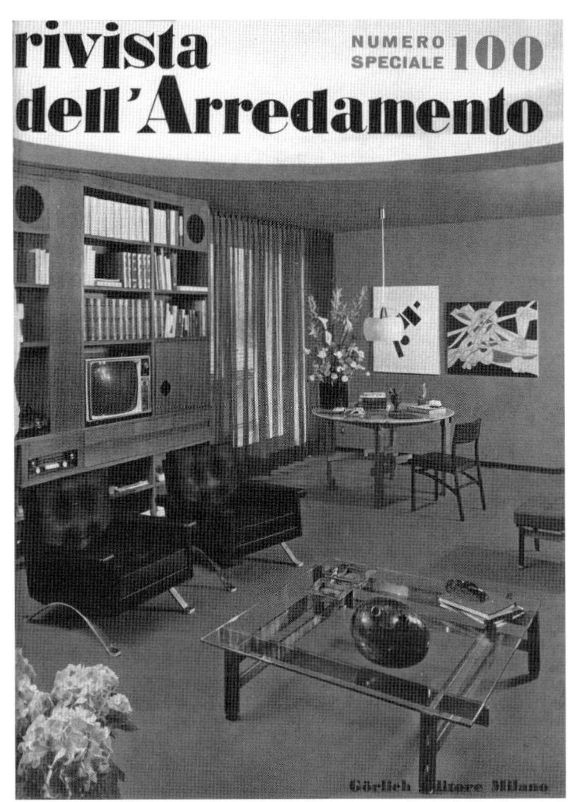

rivista dell'Arredamento

NUMERO SPECIALE 100

Görlich ditore Milano

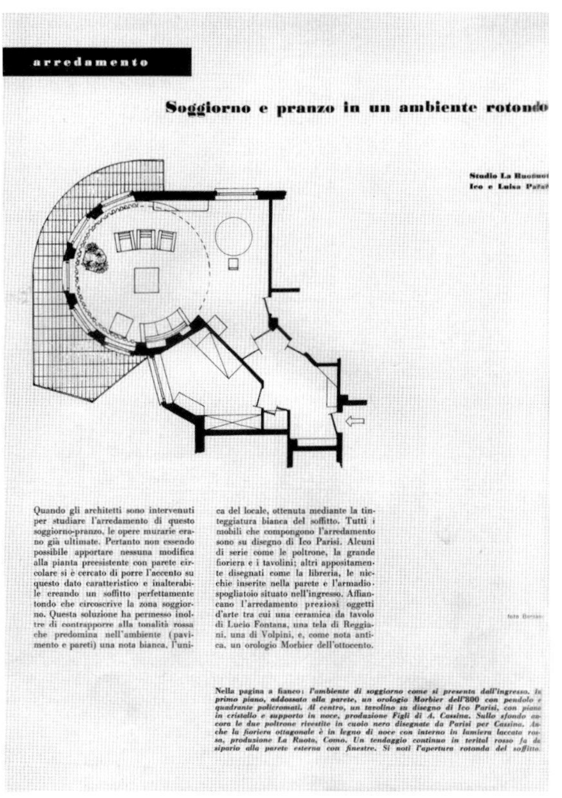

arredamento

Soggiorno e pranzo in un ambiente rotondo

Quando gli architetti sono intervenuti per studiare l'arredamento di questo soggiorno-pranzo, le opere murarie erano già ultimate. Pertanto non essendo possibile apportare nessuna modifica alla pianta preesistente con parete circolare si è cercato di porre l'accento su questo dato caratteristico e inalterabile creando un soffitto perfettamente tondo che circoscrive la zona soggiorno. Questa soluzione ha permesso inoltre di contrapporre alla tonalità rossa che predomina nell'ambiente (pavimento e pareti) una nota bianca, l'unica del locale, ottenuta mediante la tinteggiatura bianca del soffitto. Tutti i mobili che compongono l'arredamento sono su disegno di Ico Parisi. Alcuni di serie come le poltrone, la grande fioriera e i tavolini; altri appositamente disegnati come la libreria, le nicchie inserite nella parete e l'armadio-spogliatoio situato nell'ingresso. Affiancano l'arredamento preziosi oggetti d'arte tra cui una ceramica da tavolo di Lucio Fontana, una tela di Reggiani, una di Volpini, e, come nota antica, un orologio Morbier dell'ottocento.

Nella pagina a fianco: *l'ambiente di soggiorno come si presenta dall'ingresso. In primo piano, addossato alla parete, un orologio Morbier dell'800 con pendolo e quadrante policromati. Al centro, un tavolino su disegno di Ico Parisi, con piano in cristallo e supporto in noce, produzione Figli di A. Cassina. Sullo sfondo ancora le due poltrone rivestite in cuoio nero disegnate da Parisi per Cassina. Anche la fioriera ottagonale è in legno di noce con interno in lamiera laccata rossa, produzione La Ruota, Como. Un tendaggio continuo in terital rosso fa da sipario alla parete esterna con finestre. Si noti l'apertura rotonda del soffitto.*

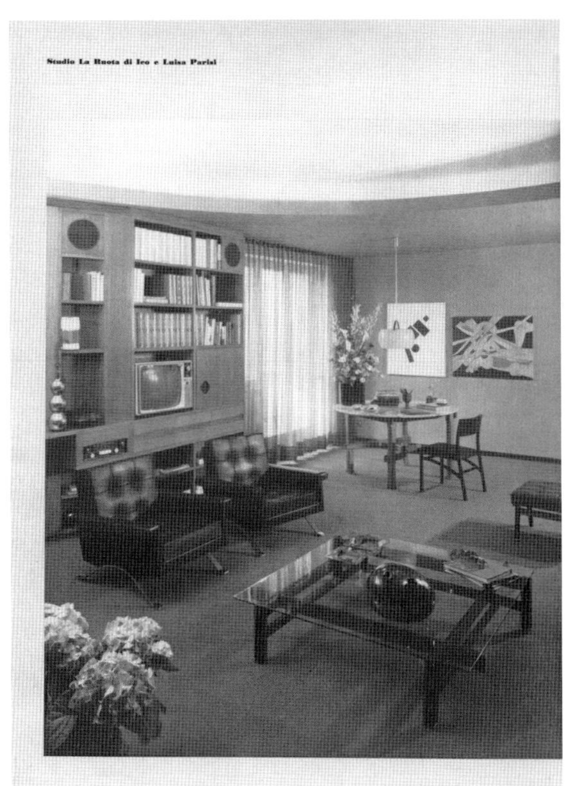

Studio La Ruota di Ico e Luisa Parisi

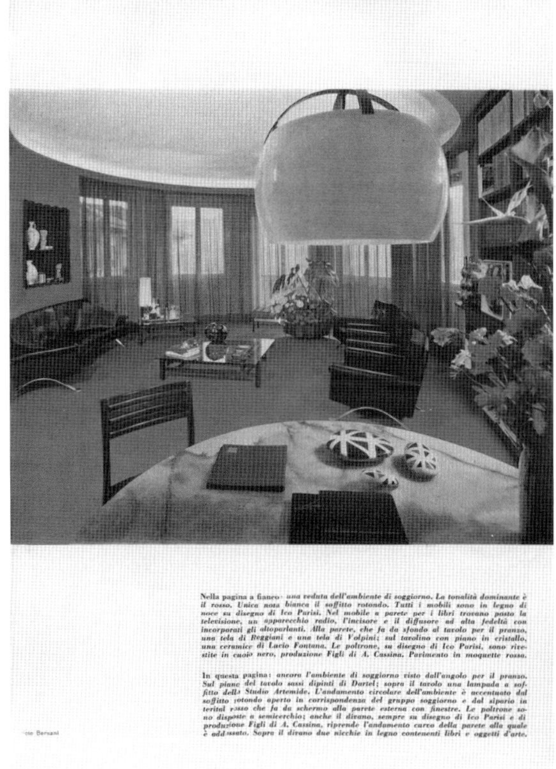

Nella pagina a fianco: *una veduta dell'ambiente di soggiorno. La tonalità dominante è il rosso. Unica nota bianca il soffitto rotondo. Tutti i mobili sono in legno di noce su disegno di Ico Parisi. Nel mobile a parete per i libri trovano posto la televisione, un apparecchio radio, l'incisore e il diffusore ad alta fedeltà con incorporati gli altoparlanti. Alla parete, che fa da sfondo al tavolo per il pranzo, una tela di Reggiani e una tela di Volpini; sul tavolino con piano in cristallo, una ceramica di Lucio Fontana. Le poltrone, su disegno di Ico Parisi, sono rivestite in cuoio nero, produzione Figli di A. Cassina. Pavimento in moquette rossa.*

In questa pagina: *ancora l'ambiente di soggiorno visto dall'angolo per il pranzo. Sul piano del tavolo sassi dipinti di Dartel; sopra il tavolo una lampada a soffitto dello Studio Artemide. L'andamento circolare dell'ambiente è accentuato dal soffitto rotondo aperto in corrispondenza del gruppo soggiorno e dal sipario in terital rosso che fa da schermo alla parete esterna con finestre. Le poltrone sono disposte a semicerchio; anche il divano, sempre su disegno di Ico Parisi e di produzione Figli di A. Cassina, riprende l'andamento curvo della parete alla quale è addossato. Sopra il divano due nicchie in legno contenenti libri e oggetti d'arte.*

Furniture by Ico Parisi with a ceramic by Fontana published in *La rivista dell'arredamento*, special number 100, April 1963

of holes in Fontana's are formally purposeful, like a code, with a casual but not to be ignored connection with the punched cards and tapes of popular cybernetics iconography. The structure of his paintings is undoubtedly simple."[14]
But the role of Damiano – who always remained in contact with Fontana, both as a collector (he would purchase around eighty works from the artist until 1968) and as a friend and great admirer of his work – went far beyond mere support or help in translating critical books from English: following the artist's success at the Venice Biennale, witnessing Fontana's further growth especially as far as the very new *tagli* were concerned, Damiano obtained a contract for a world exclusive with Mc Robert & Tunnard: he personally acted as a mediator in drawing up the contract and in managing the artist's business relationships in the Anglo-Saxon world. Fontana's solo exhibition at Mc Robert & Tunnard's took place from 12th October to 5th November 1960 and was introduced by Alloway; for the first time in London, it focused on the *tagli*.
Guided by Damiano's quick wit and firm will to promote Fontana on an international level, other exhibitions would follow the first one, among which the renowned *Ten paintings from Venice* at Martha Jackson's in New York – Fontana's debut in the city in 1961 – his solo exhibition in Leverkusen, curated by Udo Kultermann, displaying Damiano's whole collection and made possible by the manager's contacts with the German museum.
Thus, the UK was the bridgehead of the artist's first international diffusion between the late 1950s and early 1960s, alongside the important German axis nurtured by Fontana's relationships with the young members of the Zero group (Heinz Mack and Otto Piene) and as an alternative to the French scene, which, on the other hand, became preferred by gallery owner Carlo Cardazzo since 1959. As a matter of fact, the relationship between Cardazzo and the Stadler gallery should not be overlooked, in the framework of the presentation of the new series of the *tagli*, exhibited to the Milanese public in February 1959 at the Naviglio and then, in March, at the Parisian gallery owner's, with the support of Michel Tapié's influential critical interpretation. Indeed, this first appearance – which led the artist to complain, as it perhaps could have been better arranged, since Fontana inadvertently found himself sharing the gallery with South African artist Christo Coetzee – confirmed a still informal interpretation of the artist, supported by Tapié: the *taglio* as a laceration and a wound.[15] On the other hand, the introduction to the subsequent exhibition of the *tagli* in 1960, in London, edited by Alloway, stated that, "Fontana is the opposite of hermetic: he is mercurial and outgoing but he is guarded from disappearing into the gulf of sociability which threatens modern Italian artist by a protective core of indifference."[16]
Fontana's first exhibition *Ten paintings of Venice* in New York at Martha Jackson's in Autumn 1961 was the expression of the synergies between Paris and London and Venice: from a critical viewpoint, Tapié drew up a monographic study called *Devenir de Fontana*, printed for Edizioni Fratelli Pozzo in Turin and displayed in the rooms of the gallery; Damiano's work as a mediator and the collaboration with gallery owners Mc Robert and Tunnard were the first driving forces of the artist's debut in New York, which proved itself to be so crucial for Fontana's success and subsequent work; finally, within this triangulation, Venice is the place of inspiration for that *Venezie* (Venices) series, presented in America and specifically created by Fontana for the exhibition *Arte e contemplazione* organised by Marinotti at Palazzo Grassi in the summer of 1961.
To conclude, it should be pointed out that, back in 1959, Charles Damiano and his wife Maria Cambiaghi donated to the Tate Gallery a *Concetto spaziale*, which they had purchased at the Venice Biennale in 1958 and which is still an essential work in the English museum's collection, with a view to urging the museum to approach Italian contemporary art. However, perhaps the time was not yet ripe and a few decades would pass before Fontana's work caught the attention of museums in the UK.

[1] Michel Tapié, *Dévenir de Fontana*, Edizioni Fratelli Pozzo, Torino 1961. The anecdote told by Tapié aims at highlighting the artist's premature reflection around space in sculpture, rather than around overcoming volume.
[2] C. Lonzi, *Autoritratto* (Bari: 1969), p. 168.
[3] L. Ponti, "Prima astratto, poi barocco, ora spaziale", in *Domus*, n. 229, IV vol., 1948, p. 36.
[4] This is the set of sculptures identified in the General Catalogue under Nos. 49 SC 3 – 49 SC 7.
[5] ASAC, Serie Arti Visive, scat. 23, fasc. F 1949–50, published in P. Campiglio (edited by), *Lucio Fontana. Lettere 1919-1968* (Milano: Edizioni Skira, 1999), p. 150.
[6] ASAC, Serie Arti Visive, scat. 23, fasc. F 1949–50.
[7] ASAC, Serie Arti Visive, scat. 38, fasc. Executive Committee, Fontana Lucio, published in P. Campiglio (ed. by), *Lucio Fontana. Lettere 1919-1968*, cit. p. 150.
[8] ASAC, Serie Arti Visive, scat. 38, fasc. Executive Committee, Fontana Lucio.
[9] ASAC, Venice, shorthand minutes, Scarpa 7, XXVI Venice Biennale. First session of the executive committee 3712/1951 and second session of the executive committee 19–20/12/1951.
[10] This incident was analysed by G. Zanchetti, *Lucio Fontana, Concetto spaziale, 1957*, in *Esercizi di Lettura* (Milano: Edizioni Skira, 2002), pp. 181–203.
[11] The exhibition also included works by Ajmone, Bacci, Birolli, Brunori, Capogrossi, Chighine, Corpora, Morandi, Moreni, Morlotti, Negri.
[12] G. Zanchetti, *Lucio Fontana, Concetto spaziale, 1957*, cit. pp. 191–98.
[13] F. Tedeschi, *L'opera di Fontana tra gli anni Cinquanta e Sessanta e la sua ricezione nell'ambiente inglese*, in *Lucio Fontana Beyond Space*, Imago art Gallery, 19th October - 16th December 2008, pp. 16–27.
[14] L. Alloway, *Paintings from Damiano Collection, ICA, London, catalogue of the exhibition*, 7th January - 7th February 1959.
[15] On that occasion, Pierre Restany wrote that, "The saddest thing is that a similar juxtaposition was imposed to Fontana for his first important exhibition in Paris. Here, Fontana is not widely known. [...] The scale of the character, his past, the openness of his research, all of this deserved a better, or at least a different presentation. All the works displayed were recent: mostly monochrome canvasses, torn by longitudinal lacerations. It is all there, in the expression of that gesture. But that gesture lost all of its greatness within Coetzee's context, such an aggressively Baroque one." P. *Restany, Fontana, Coetzee, Tàpies*, "Cimaise", 5th June, July, August 1959, p. 46, referred to in S. Bignami J. Galimberti, *Lucio Fontana e L'artventure parigina* (Scalpendi editore, 2014), p. 16.
[16] L. Alloway, *Lucio Fontana*, 12th October - 5th November (London: Mc Robert & Tunnard, 1960).

Critical Anthology

A brief critical anthology gathers a number of not easily available introductions to the first exhibitions of Lucio Fontana in London and New York, from 1957 to 1962, edited by Lawrence Alloway and Pierre Rouve. The papers are contemporary with the diffusion of the *Concetti spaziali* in the British and American contexts. The anthology contains the judgement that Alloway expressed on Fontana's works – some of which belonged to the Damiano collection – included in the collective exhibition *Between space and earth. Trends in Italian Art*, organised on the initiative of Eric Estorick and Carlo Damiano at the Marlborough Gallery in London, 4th June - 31st July 1957; it also reports the paper concerning Fontana, again edited by Alloway, in *Painting from the Damiano Collection Fontana, Dova, Crippa, Clemente*, catalogue of the exhibition at the ICA, London, 7th January - 7th February 1959; the English critic's comment on the first translation of the Technical Manifesto of Spatialism (1951), wrongly dated 1947, published in "ARK" in late 1959 or early 1960; the introduction, once again edited by Alloway, to the first exhibition of Fontana's *tagli* in London, at the show organised by Mc Roberts & Tunnard, 12th October - 5th November 1960; Pierre Rouve's essay in *Fontana paintings 1962*, Mc Robert & Tunnard, November-December 1962.

P.C.

L. Alloway, *Preface*, in *Between space and earth. Trends in Italian Art*, organized by Eric Estorick and Carlo Damiano at Galleria Marlborough, London 4 June - 31 July 1957.

[...] The movement was started by Fontana in Buenos Aires in 1946 with the publication of his *Manifiesto Blanco*. In April 1947, Fontana, back in Italy, published the first Italian manifesto on Spazialismo in Milan. Five more manifestos in the next six years established the movement with changing signatories but a constant programme. An essential part of the Spazialismo stance, growing out of a revived interest in Futurism in post-war Italy, is an admiration of Boccioni as an iconoclast and as a promoter of modernity. What the Futurists did for the motor car the spaziali propose to do for the dynamic space, microcosmic or astronomic, of modern science: 'It will not be possible to adapt to these new exigencies of the past'. 'Today we spatial artist have got away from our cities, we have broken our chrysallis, our physical limitations, and we are looking down from above, photographing the earth from rockets'. However, where the futurists were precise about the machines that made the new experiences available, the artists of Spazialismo stress the 'spatial sensation created by imagination' stimulated by new experiences, apart from the mechanical means of achieving it. Significantly one of the early meeting places of the group was the office of the Italian architects Rogers, Perossuti and Belgiojoso. Statements of the group often seem to need architecture and other media than pure painting for realisation, thus recalling the desire of many modern artists to transcend the artificial limits of art and create a new environment. This is the motive for their claim that 'we will transmit by radio and television artistic expressions of a new kind'. 'With the resources of modern science we will cause to appear in the sky:

artificial forms,
rainbows of wonder,
luminous writing'.

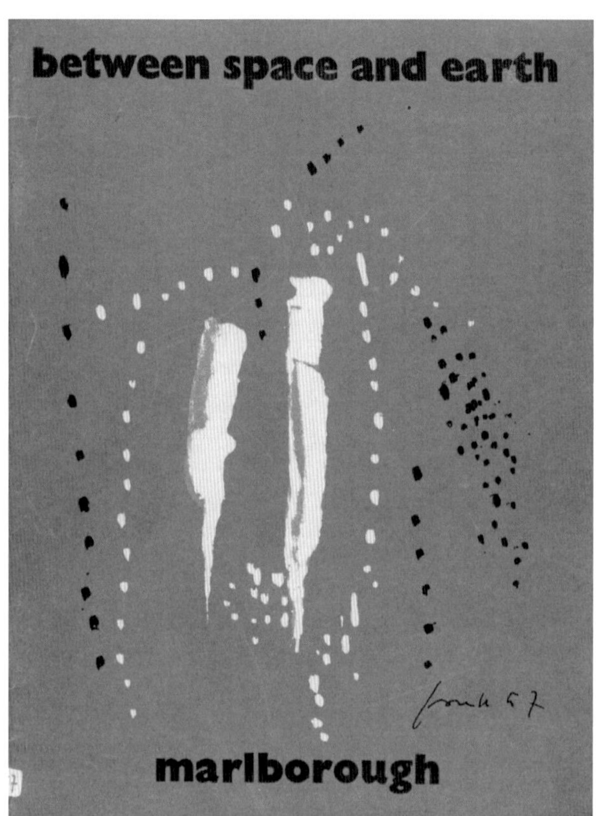

Between space and earth. Trends in Italian Art, Galleria Marlborough, London, 4 June - 31 July 1957

If not in the sky, then on canvas. Space is what these artists aspire to, but they give it the earthly form of easel painting. Though this optimistic programme could not be achieved literally by painters, it is evidence of the intention of these artists to create a style which does not reject the new visual conventions of science. The spaziali reject both the categories of geometric abstraction and of 'terrestrial' realism. In their place they aim to create an art close to aspects of science, without reducing art to the role of illustrations to science. The similarities of art and science proclaimed in the manifestos – 'the conquests of science are now at the service of the art we profess' – give to painters a world without horizons a world in which indeterminate spaces can be symbolised by the act of painting. Turbulent brush strokes become a metaphor of solar turbulence (splashes as sunspots) and gestures with the brush are read as a cosmic *graffiti*.

Fontana is the only artist in the group to have realised the technical programme of Spazialismo – namely, the use of materials newer than oil paint or bronze, as in his perforated reliefs and the reliefs studied with mineral forms, somewhere between constructivism and costume jewellery. In these works he constructs on the surface of his reliefs so that space may be defined as the distance between points on a plane rather than as an illusion of recession. Capogrossi in his paintings of signs stretched in bands across the canvas is also concerned, as the titles of the pictures prove, wit 'surfaces'. This emphasis on the surface of the picture plane is common to a great deal of modern art: its novelty in these two cases is in the sense of space *across* the surface, from point to point, rather than, as in Gauguin or Matisse, the translation of the world into something at flat.

Bacci and Gino Morandi elaborate the surface of their paintings with a sensuous burden of paint which dissolves into a range of amorphous images, evocative within decorative limits of 'the new landscape' of science. Once again, control is essential for the paint must be prevented from forming shapes and figures which would limit the possibilities of imagination faced with mysterious space.

L. Alloway, *Paintings of Damiano Collection*, Istitute of Contemporary Arts, London, January 1959, s.p.

These paintings from the Damiano Collection have been selected with the purpose of showing some of the best work by three artists of the Spazialismo group which has been more talked about than seen in London. To the group of Fontana, Crippa, and Dova has been added Jacques Clemente whose work represents, along with Crippa's and Dova's later works (not in an exhibition), a counter-current to Spazialismo.
The Spazialismo mouvement was started in Italy in 1947, based on a manifesto written the previous year by Fontana. A tenet of the group, which connects with Milanese interests as a whole, was the link between art and science, one form of which was a demand for new materials. In practise this often took the form of an unconventional use of traditional media. On the iconographic level there are connections between the symbolic presentations of science and the artist's imagery. Crippa's graphism touches on 'the world of the atom', for exemple, and Dova's automatism invokes both large (galatic) and small (visceral) spaces.
Fontana is an artist who has not received proper recognitions. Known for his ceramics and design projects at the Triennale, he is also a most important painter, with a sense of materials that is both spectacular and disciplined. Even when he studs his pictures with fragments of shining ceramincs, a lush device, he makes a curt demostration of order. Austerity continually checks his jewel-scattering hand. The shards that rise in front of the surface are countered by cuts into and throught the picture surface. Fontana does this not by making a raised paste and incising it but by piercing the picture plane. This has the function of dramatising the surface, either the taut thinness of canvas, with fraying edges, or the rigidity of board which carries cleaner, deeper holes. (Fontana punctured his pictures as early as 1949 which makes him a probable influence on the younger, better know, Tàpies). Holes in pictures are usually a sign of ruin, but the patterns of holes in Fontana's are formally purposeful, like a code, with a casual but not to be ignored connection with the punched cards and tapes of popular cybernetics iconography. The format of this paintings is resolutely simple which works for him because of his razor-fine feeling for the siting of forms and their edge-relations. [...]

Lawrence Alloway commentary of "Technical Manifesto given at the 1st International Congress Of Proportion at the IXth Triennale, Milan 1947", in *Ark*, 1959 ca.

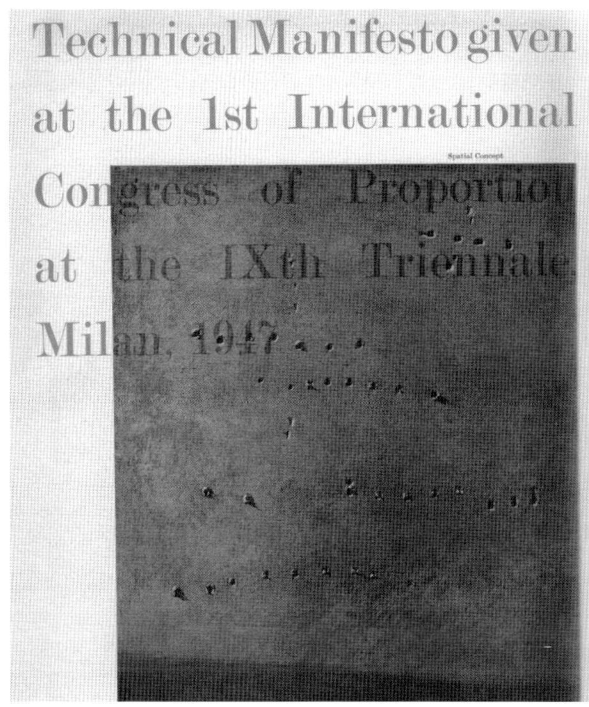

"Technical Manifesto given at the 1st International Congress Of Proportion at the IXth Triennale, Milan 1947", in *Ark*, 1959

An avant-garde is an ideas-élite but today its ideas [like everybody's] circulate so rapidly that they get separeted from their originators. Spazialismo is a case in point. The term has been used to promote an ill-assorted group of Italian painters, but it is essentialy the property of one man, Lucio Fontana [b. 1899]. Fontana is the only artist who fits the requirements of his own technical manifesto [printed below].

Fontana believes [like so many of the avant-garde] in the disappearance of easel painting. Since 1949, he has written, 'I called all my paintings spatial concepts', thus, they are the second manifesto of Spazialismo, 1948, it was claimed the 'with the resources of modern science we will cause to appear in the sky: artifical forms, rainbows of wonder, luminous writing'. The only works that this fits are Fontana's ceilings of the early fiftes, in which he used neon in multi-directional arrow-head forms and in fluent?, snaky tangles. In one he pierced holes in a suspended ceiling, shaped like a huge, flat holly leaf. These environmental works going on overhead, dancing on the ceiling, pass 'beyond painting' into the field of industrial design. The majority of this spatial concepts, however, are phisically easel paintigs [linen mounted on stretchers, boards] though he treats them more widly than the other so-called Spazialist artistis.

Easel painting is the most permissive of all art forms, permitting extremes of experiment and probably Fontana is not, as he thinks, destroying easel painting but enlarging its means. He scatters ceramic chips across the surface, like 'a throw of the dice': he sprinkles powdered metal on impasted paint masses; and he makes his famous holes, which are clean or frayed, according to the surface and the tool.

What is the function of the holes, which he has been making since 1949? They are usually in learnable patterns so that that act as a kind of drawing by negative; like holes in a punched card, like bullet holes in a wall, the holes carry information. The surface as implacably given, the carrier if the massage, has been a costituent fat of modern art since Gauguin and Mallarmé. Fontana put things on the surface: ceramics or patches of canvas; he opens up the surface by punched holes and, more recently, by slashes. The flatness of the picture is not an area into which the world must be sandwiched [as in the flat-pattern days of the contrary, the physical area in which the artist works, marking his decisions and discoveries. Fontana's incisive subtle, economical style, with occasional lush outbursts, reveals a mastery of surface tension that only Mathieu and Dubuffet can match in Europe. Fontana's linking of the flat picture plane with a specifically 'modern' space has connections with other modern art. Malewitsch [in his Bauhausbucher, no. 11, 1927] criticized Futurism for its retention of the horizon, comparing it with horizon-free Supermatism. He printed photographs of vertical [up] shots of formations of planes in flight and vertical [down] photographs of the earth.

L. Alloway, *Fontana*, McRoberts & Tunnard Gallery, London, 12 October - 5 November 1960

Now the 'modern' art has a substantial history behind it, it is possible to begin sorting out what really happened. We can see, for example, that some of the artists who got caught up on the rapid style-changes and experimental outlook of modern art did not really belong there. Hence critical appraisal of modern art is discovering covert classism in unexpected places traditional faces under modern hats. But the reverse is also true: certaint artists, Boccioni and Picabia, for example, were clearly in their element, destined by temperament as well as by art history, to celebrate the ways in which modern art is unlike the art of the past. Lucio Fontana is clearly of this company – a man on edge with no nostalgia for repose; restless, with no regret for lost certainties.

Fontana, by character and by decision, is a pure avant-garde type, in the sense that renewal is his constat aim. He does not even guard his own gifts, which other modern artists have treasured as the last and unexpendable convention. He is willing to call in doubt his own work, to consign suddenly what he is doing to "the past". The collection of his work in the Palazzo Centrale in the Venice Biennale of 1958, for example, contained some of his most grave and beautiful works. Immediately afterwards he cancelled their rich aestethic with his first cuts, in which he slit the throats of simply dyed canvasses. This peremptory gesture, like moments in Picasso's development, was an espression of his impatience to pursue a new theme. What began as a gesture has been continued and estended as a basic part of Fontana's oeuvre.

Speed of execution, related to freshness of appearance, is precious to Fontana. He is opposed to the idea of the work of art as a palce in which anguished creation leaves its traces, as in Giacometti or de Kooning. He likes the clear, incisive sign. Like Whistler in this respect (who believed the all record of effort must be banished form art) or Mathieu, he aims for the pure, unqualified mark. In Fontana's creative act delay is not the sign of meditation but of forgetfulness and failure. Centred patches of crusty material, scattered trails of ceramic chips, calligraphic streaks and flicks, neat perforations – directional as a code, or stark as a wound, all are made with a maximum vigour and semplicity.

Avant-garde, too, is Fontana's way of working in an ambiguous medium. The problematic is always the territory of the avant-garde and there is a problem at the heart of Fontana's work. This problem has nothing to do with the resolving of complex pictorial tensions in the act of working, as in Hans Hofmann, for exemple. Fontana's problem is not part of the process of creation; it is presented to us with the finished work itself, as an inherent ambiguity. Is his work painting or relief-sculpture? The artist himself does not regard it as either exactly and since 1949 has called his work "spatial concepts". It is relevant to be reminded here that is Fontana is famous in Milan not only for his avant-garde work but also for his ceramincs, much prized as elegant ornaments. Ever since Art Nouveau modern artists have made the decorative arts expressive and the expressive arts decorative. This trascendence of the traditional bounfaries of fine and applied arts seems to underlie the ambiguous status of the spatial concepts. Certainly it is to Fontana's liking to work in a tecnicque unconcluded by traditional definitions.

The avant-gardes of the 20th century art have, on one hand, a traditional link with Bohemias and underworlds (as in the Beats of the 50's) or, on the other hand, a sympatethic link with the city and with

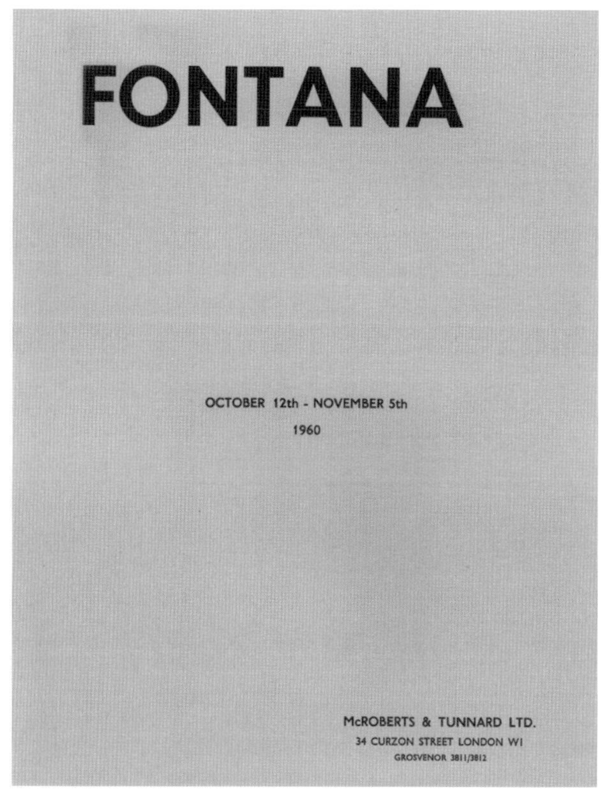

Fontana, McRoberts & Tunnard Gallery, London, 12 October - 5 November 1960

the industry. Fontana's ideal company is clear from his manifestos of Spazialismo. This movement, which he formulated in 1946, pronounced his acceptance of modern life. In the Technical Manifesto of Spazialismo (1949), the longest formal account Fontana has given of his ideas, he wrote: "The discovery of new physical power, the conquest of matter and space, gradually impose on man conditions which have never existed before. The application of these discoveries to the various forms of life brings about a substantial trasformation in our ways of thinking. The painted surface, the rected stone, no longer have a meaning".

This typically Milanese pleasure in science and technology (Milano is the home of both Futurism and the Triennale) does not link Fontana's spatial concepts with a specifically technological content. On the contrary, his works have a Pompeian freshness and sense of creation as play. What it does do, however, and this essential to our understanding of his character, is to root his personal ebullience in a wide sense of "the ever-changing conditions of life". Fontana is the opposit of hermetic: he is mercurial and outgoing, but he is guarded from disappearing into the gulf of sociability which threatens modern Italian artists by a protective core of indifference. His manifestos, for exemple, were adopted to cover a large and ill-assorted group of Italian painters none of whom, by 1956, fitted any of Fontana's definitions. But Fontana gave no sign of minding, and this indifference, not to his contemporaries but to his own part, as represented by Spazialismo, is typical of the man. In England the idea of the avant-garde has been less discussed and less exemplified than in any other country. One reason for this is that most of our modern painters have not been temperamentally of the phoenix-kind. They have been more cerned with the enrichment of their original gifts than with gambling on renewal, which of course, has its dangeres as well as its rewards. A lobatomised innocence of a foot-hold on a new land? It can go either way. Equally, however, over estimation of the worth of one's present talent and past performance may be prudent, but it can become boring. Fontana, however, has a rigorous welcome for the future and he makes of renewal a principle. From his work it is clear that for Fotnana renewal is the medium of his art.

P. Rouve, *Fontana Pantings 1962*,
McRoberts & Tunnard Gallery, London,
November 1962

Fontana furrows the calm acre of the canvas and twists the tenderness of colour into a sudden convulsion of rage. And the scar stares, eye of the void. We shudder: is this the message of a modern Prometheus, chained to the rock of despair, resolved to unmask the ultimate nullity of our existence? We wonder: no mushroom cloud casts its dark shadow on Fontana's limpid canvases. We question: is the artist blissfully unaware of the tragic immensity inherent in these statements uttered with such disconcerting ease? And the slow gestation of our answer reveals the complex core of Fontana's art.

The metaphysical charge of the martyred matter is hardly beyond the reach of his remarkably lucid mind. Still he refuses to state it in grim pedantic terms – perhaps because his experience of our common predicament bears quite a different stamp. He did not reach this intuition of cosmic cataclysm at the end of drab logical deductions and even less at the start of extrovert emotional explosions. He stumbled upon it in the middle of his play with existence, privilege of the few for whom wisdom and innocence are inseparable playmates.

Playfulness is not physiological flippancy, it is the serene side of the spirit. Fontana unravels this forgotten truth from underneath huge heaps of calvinist curses and reminds us that the play is neither biological necessity nor moral verdict: it is an existential evidence. Stripped from all moralizing incrustations, the word stands out in all its semantic ambiguity. We play the play: the verb is also a noun, action is also outcome, motion is also rest. This deep duality may well be the best introduction to the condensed amplitude of Fontana's work.

It is therefore clear that neither the quiet premeditation of the colour nor the lightning wound on the canvas are what they seem. There are no arbitrary gestures in Fontana's art, only acts. And acts are always imbued with a sense of finality. Gestures ramble. Acts know where they are going, even when that knowledge does not fit our discursive moulds. Chance affects them as it intervenes in a game, not as it presides over the unfurling of chaos. All improvisations respect the rules of the game: and the name of this game is life.

Fontana Pantings 1962, McRoberts & Tunnard Gallery, London, November 1962

This conformity to the hidden inflections of the human situation is also an outburst of non-conformist

defiance. In his sophisticated simplicity, Fontana scorns both those who still believe that art is *quod visum placet* and those who accept only what displeases the sight. But his defiance goes much deeper and questions our basic approach to abstract art.
Our eyes have been patiently trained to look, in non figurative paintings, for structures and not for spectacles, for statements and not for delights. Suddenly Fontana makes us once again spectators and not commentators. These baffling blends of tactile coagulations and optical exquisiteness begin by asserting their physical presence – concrete, tangible, not very different from that of any Renaissance relief. And so Fontana's works, heralds of spatial revolt, start as peaceful inhabitants of the Euclidian universe – as its most sincere denizens. There, distances are material, measurable, objective: the pierced canvas is the most real definition of space. Fontana is the only realist. But these scientifically measurable spaces are not lifeless topographies: for all its concrete assertion, this is not the space of geometry, it is the emotional space to be evaluated not in inches, but in heart-beats. Fontana has forced us to live what we would have only measured. And we are then compelled to realize that geometry has been mere rational abstraction: the intangible space scanned by our sensations is concrete, parcel of our pulse, part of our reality, salt of our existence. Fontana is the real realist.
Of course, much has been said about the spatial commitment of his work and people have come to believe that he is illustrating the poetic cosmogony of Cyrano de Bergerac who thought that all stars were holes in a dark firmament filtering some eternal light stored in the infinite. Perhaps the time has come to stress that Fontana is less interested in spacemen and their heights than in the space of man and its depth. He may have found visual assonances between astral macrocosms and existential microcosms – but he has mapped our anguish, not the star-sprinkled sky.
And if we are to credit him with a cosmogony, we shall discover that for him all light is in the human side of the celestial vault. Beyond is darkness. The infinity is infinite nothingness. To catch a glimpse of it, is to shudder in despair. Perhaps this is why there, is such condensation of terror around these craters of distress opening in the consoling calm of the colour. But this chromatic exquisiteness is not an accident. It is the hallmark of modern man playing at hope.

Works

I CAVALLI CHE SEGUONO LA VITTORIA (BOZZETTO) [HORSES FOLLOWING VICTORY (MODEL)], 1936

Bronze
This work is unique
52 × 60 × 25 cm. (20 1/2 × 23 5/8 × 9 7/8 in.)

Provenance
Private collection, Milan

Exhibitions
Milan, Museo della Permanente, *Lucio Fontana e Milano*, 11 October - 17 November 1996, pp. 54-152, no. 8
Milan, Triennale di Milano, *Centenario di Lucio Fontana. Cinque Mostre a Milano. Lucio Fontana, la Triennale, la Luce*, 23 April - 30 June 1999, pp. 170-354, no. II, 14
Leeds, Henry Moore Institute; Rovereto, MART, *Dead Language Sculpture. Sculpture from Fascist Italy; Scultura Lingua Morta: Scultura nell'Italia Fascista*, 2003, p. 98, no. 5

Bibliography
P. Campiglio, *Lucio Fontana. La Scuola Architettonica degli Anni Trenta*, Ilisso, Nuoro 1995, pp. 83-84, no. 46
E. Crispolti, *Fontana*, Charta, Milan 1999, pp. 114, 115, no. 44
E. Crispolti, *Lucio Fontana, Catalogo Ragionato di Sculture, Dipinti, Ambientazioni*, vol. II, Edizioni Skira, Milan 2006, p. 935, no. 36 A 5

Between 1935 and 1936, the group of architects and artists led by Edoardo Persico, with Giancarlo Palanti, Marcello Nizzoli and Lucio Fontana, won the competition to decorate the *Salone d'Onore* (Main Hall) in the VI Milan Triennale opened in May 1936. The hall was the highest point of symbolic concentration in the entire official exhibition and had been designed by Persico with a noble tone, by adopting a continuous rhythm of high wings encapsulating – in an abstract sense – the idea of ancient colonnade.
The total white environment, separated by the rest of the building, was artificially lit and emanated a ghostly dim light. Fontana imagined, within the rational space designed by Persico, a remarkable sculptural group made of plaster on a high base, formed by an allegorical figure moving forward in the foreground, representing Fascist Italy, followed by an ancient symbol of energy and dynamism: two prancing horses. However, the outcome of the occupation campaign in Ethiopia, during the months of preparation of the exhibition, imposed by order of the authorities to change the name of the work into *Vittoria* (Victory) and forced the artist to engrave a sentence by Mussolini in the base of the group. A set of photomontages by Nizzoli, showing portraits of Roman emperors at the entrance, gave to the environment the official tone requested by the client, with modern techniques.
The sketch for the horses, in patinated bronze, which was presented by Fontana as a proof for the commission, states the original aim of the artist of adopting an abstract colour (a black or white achromia) over a representative basis with a strong dynamical synthesis, highlighting the issue of identity between abstraction and representation. The ancient theme of the prancing horse as a symbol for energy and dynamism – appreciated by Futurists – is personally reinterpreted by Fontana as an emblem of a moving mass that develops in space, since his first sculptures in the 1930s; later on, the prancing horse, the so-called '*caballo loco*', would remain one of the artist's favourite themes for his ceramic works, the symbol of irrational energy, the emblem of a pure display of strength in movement, almost a memory of his past as a '*gaucho*' in the Argentine pampas.

Here is a note by Enrico Crispolti from the last *Lucio Fontana. Catalogo Ragionato di Sculture, Dipinti, Ambientazioni*, Skira editore 2006, p. 53
[...] During these years, after his collaboration with architects in the early 1930s, his interest as a sculptor in working with architecture was enriched by new and more substantial experiences, remaining a constant part of his activity and to some extent actually constituting its most complex parameter.
[...] In the first half of 1936 Fontana produced the large sculptural group for the *Salone della Vittoria* at the 5th Milan Triennale (Victory followed by prancing horses, in plaster, 6 m high). It was a notable example of environmental characterization in Italian Rationalist Architecture, "simple limit of space in which to erect a completely independent and original work," Edoardo Persico wrote in his report in February 1936. The work was, in fact, the group sculpted by Fontana, the only figurative intervention in the purity of the architectural context, characterized by walls made of repeated pillars lit from behind. [...] Fontana therefore took part with his own specific mechanical means in that event of clean and rational monumentality, openly anti-rhetorical and therefore opposed to the triumphalism that prevailed in the official architecture of the fascist regime, post-20th century but now also often mixed with rationalism.

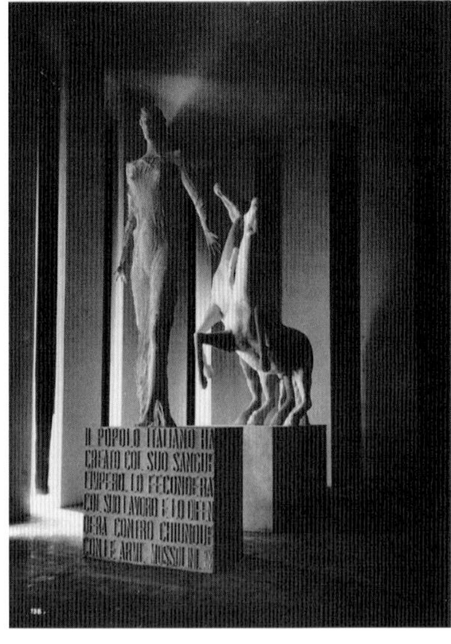

Lucio Fontana, *Vittoria*, chalk,
h. 500 cm ca.
Realized for the Salone della Vittoria
at VI Triennale of Milan, now destroyed

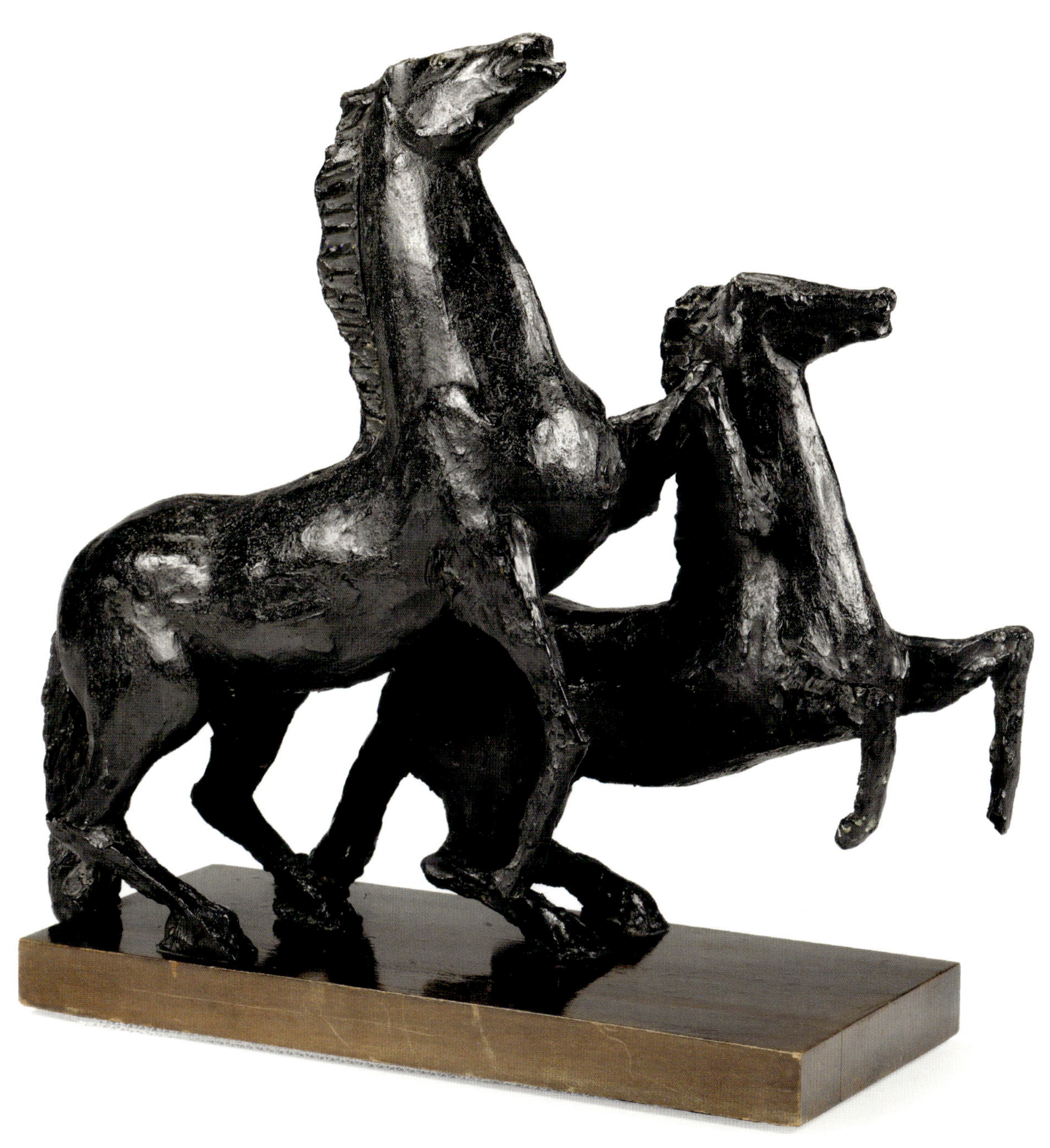

CAVALLO [HORSE], 1936

Glazed ceramic on wooden base
52 × 51 × 33 cm. (20 1/2 × 20 × 13 in.)

Provenance
Private collection, Milan

Exhibitions
Milan, Museo della Permanente, *Lucio Fontana e Milano*, 11 October - 17 November 1996, pp. 94-152, no. 9

Bibliography
E. Crispolti, *Lucio Fontana, Catalogo Ragionato di Sculture, Dipinti, Ambientazioni*, Edizioni Skira, Milan 2006, vol. I, p. 166, no. 36 SC 10

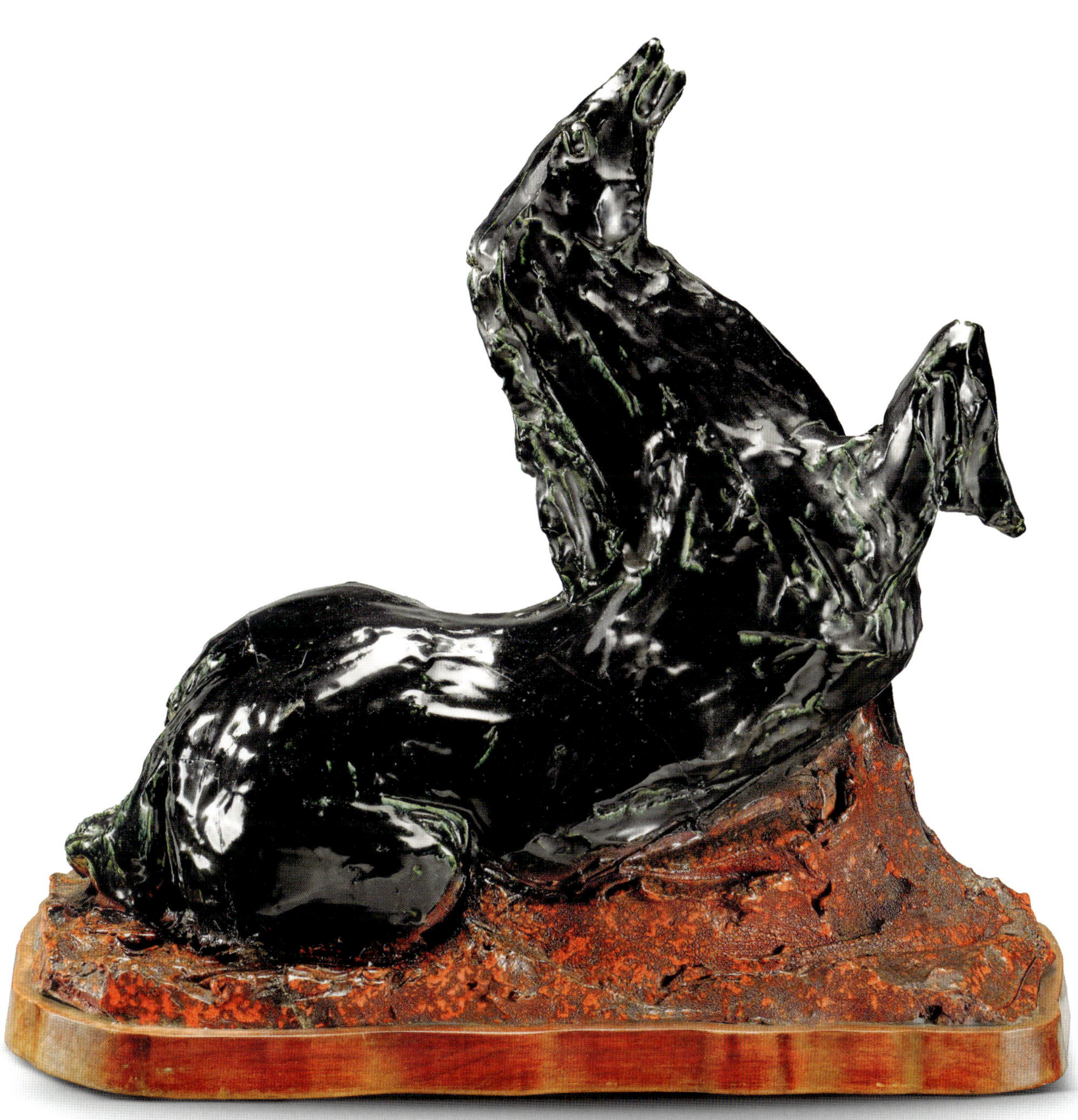

MADONNA CON BAMBINO
[MADONNA WITH CHILD], C. 1950-55

Signed with initials *l. f.* on the base
Painted and glazed ceramic
40 × 17 × 20 cm. (15 3/4 × 6 3/4 × 7 7/8 in.)

Provenance
Private collection, Legnano (Milan)

This work is registered in the *Archivio della Fondazione Lucio Fontana, Milan* under number 250/2.

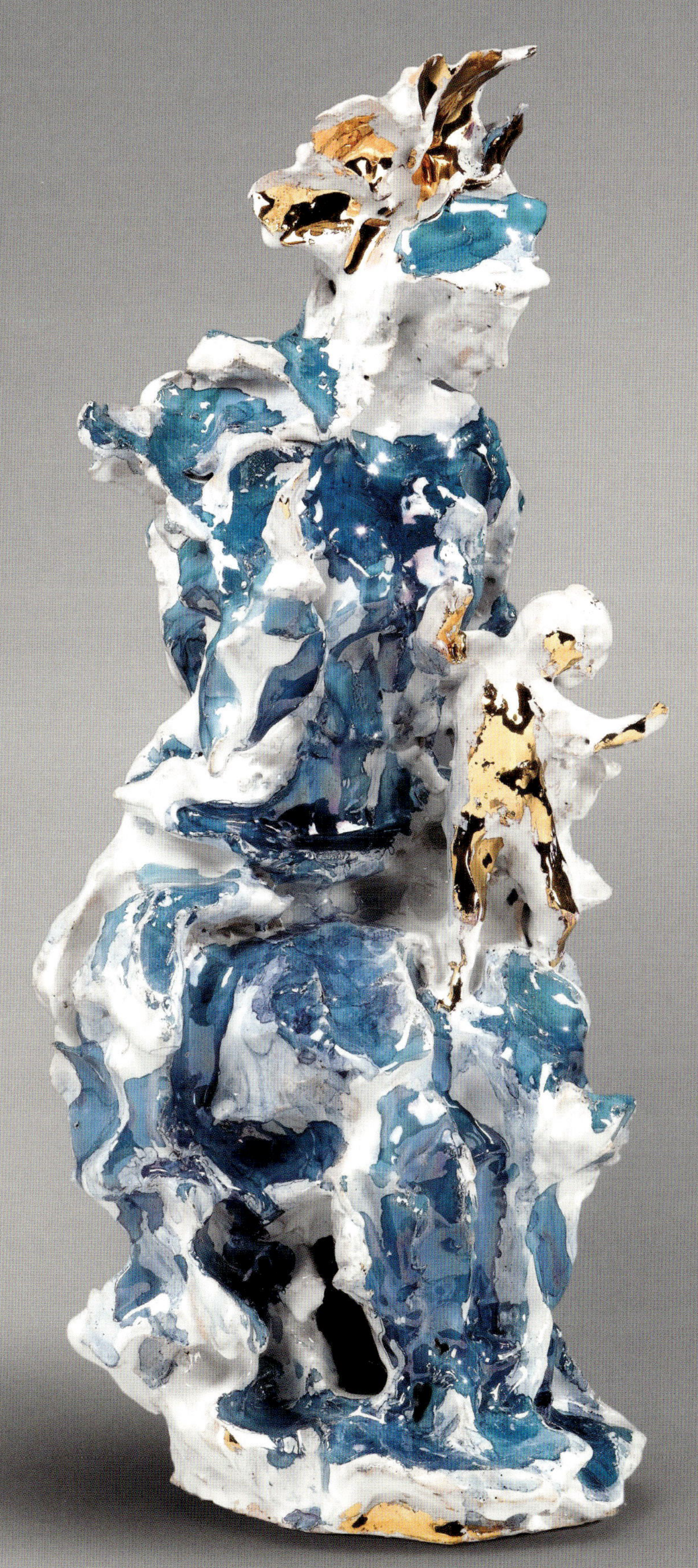

BALLERINA [BALLERINA], 1952

Signed and dated *l. Fontana / 52* on the upper edge of the base; signed with initials *L.F.* on the lower edge of the base
Painted ceramic
91 × 41 × 32.5 cm. (35 7/8 × 16 1/8 × 12 3/4 in.)

Provenance
Private collection, Trivero (Vercelli)

Exhibitions
Madrid, Palacio del Reitiro, *Exposicion de Arte Italiano Contemporaneo*, Biennal Hispano-Americana de Arte, May - June 1955, p. 50, no. 7

Bibliography
E. Crispolti, *Lucio Fontana, Catalogo Generale*, Edizioni Electa, Milan 1986, vol. I, p. 158, no. 52 SC 18
E. Crispolti, *Lucio Fontana, Catalogo Ragionato di Sculture, Dipinti, Ambientazioni*, Edizioni Skira, Milan 2006, vol. I, p. 298, no. 52 SC 18

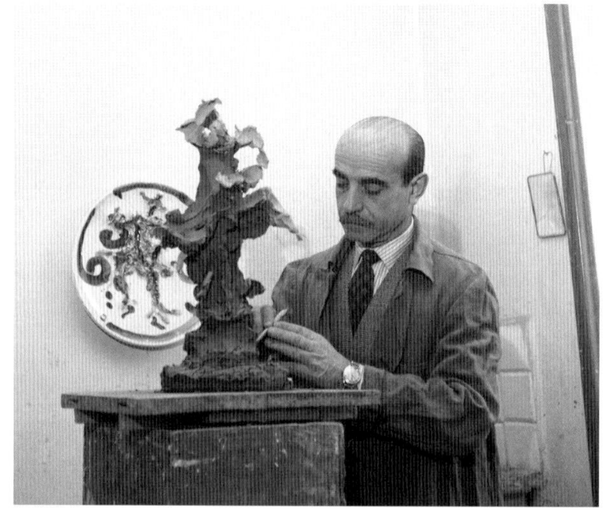

Lucio Fontana sculpting *Ballerina* in his studio

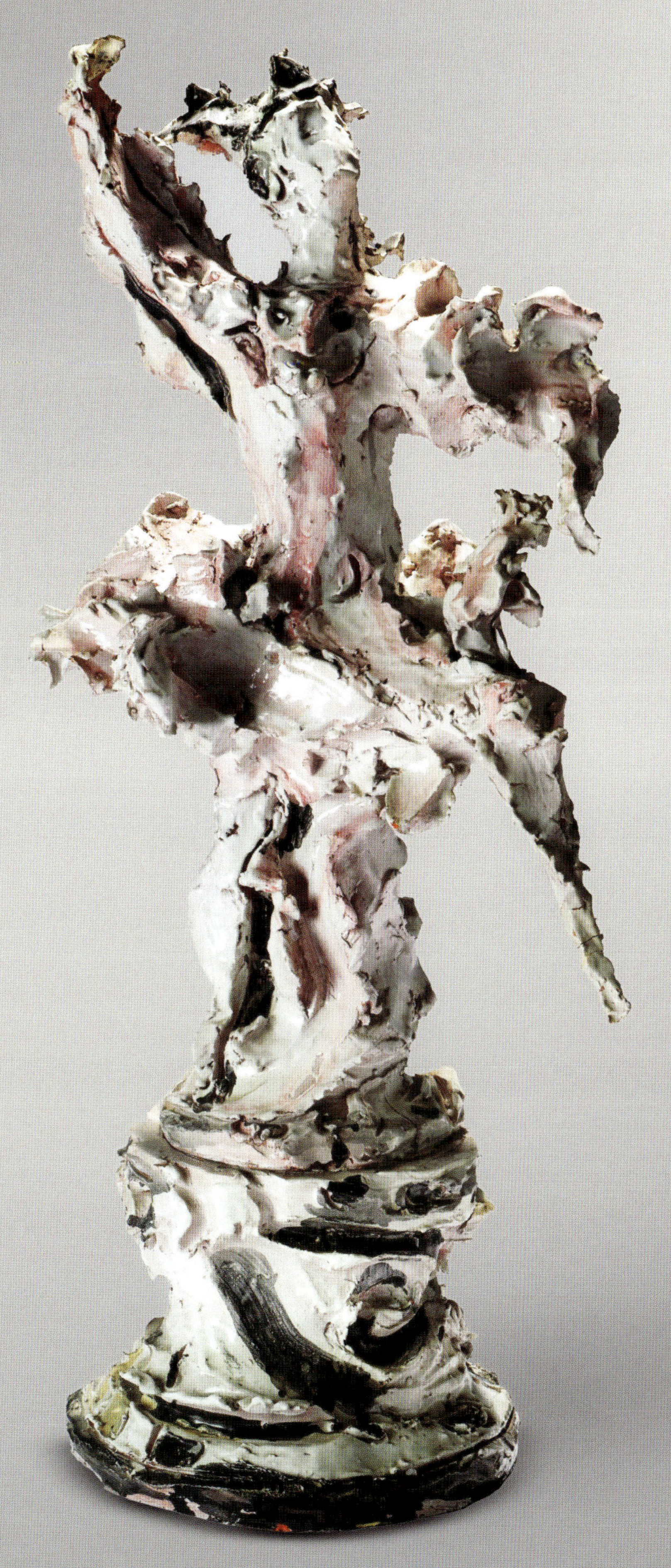

BASE PER TAVOLO CON DECORAZIONI FLOREALI E FIGURA FEMMINILE [TABLE BASE WITH FLORAL DECORATIONS AND FEMALE FIGURE], 1952

Signed and dated *l. Fontana '52* on the base
Painted terracotta
64 × 36 × 36 cm. (25 1/4 × 14 1/8 × 14 1/8 in.)

Provenance
Private collection, Milan

This work is registered in the *Archivio della Fondazione Lucio Fontana, Milan* under number *3724/1*.

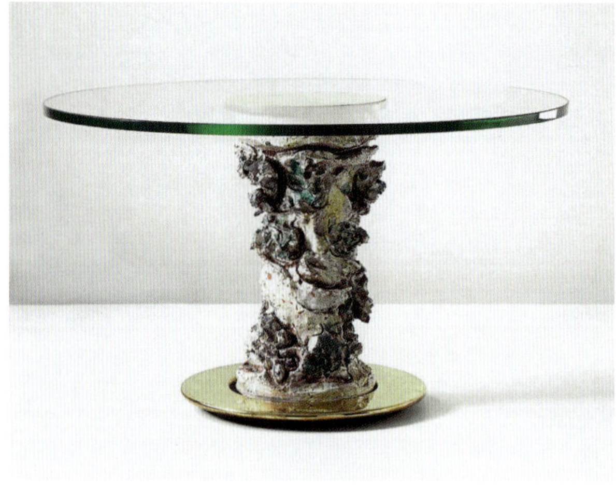

Picture of another model

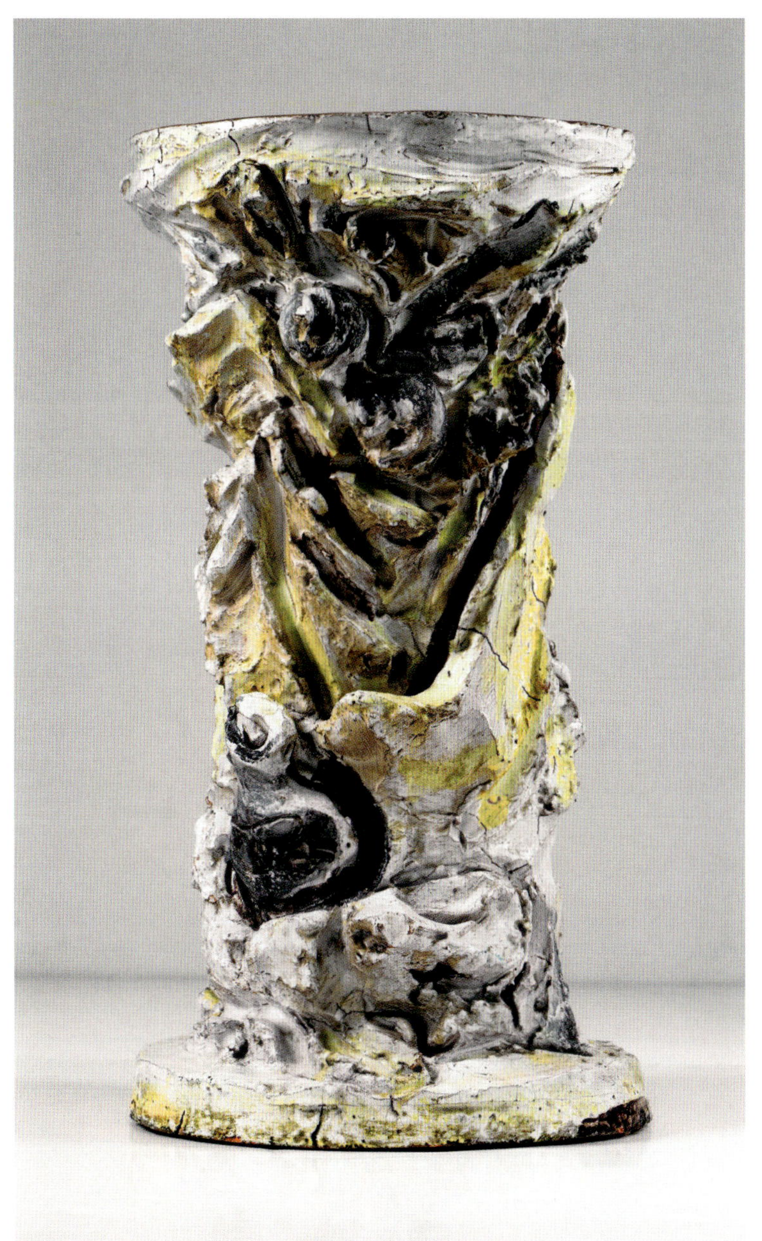

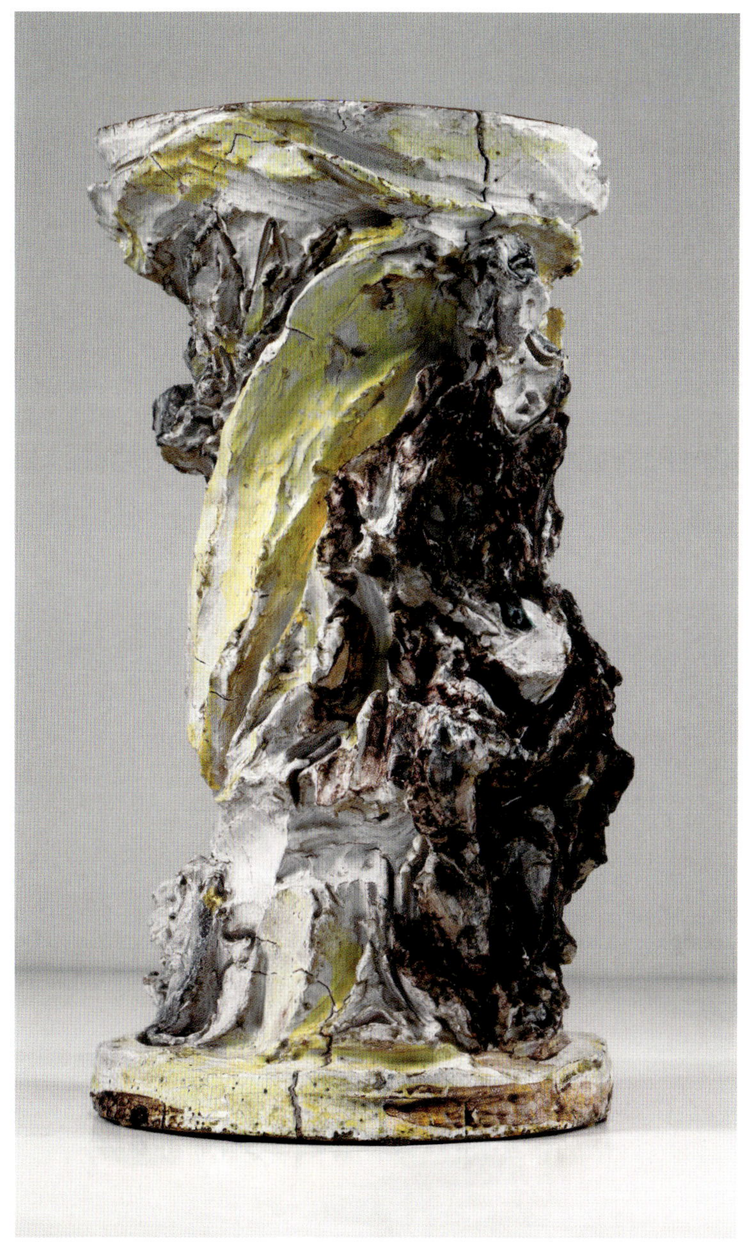

CONCETTO SPAZIALE
[SPATIAL CONCEPT], 1954

Incised with signature and date *l. fontana 54*
on the lower right
Painted terracotta with graffiti
25 × 31 cm. (9 7/8 × 12 1/4 in.)

Provenance
Private collection, Milan

Exhibitions
Milan, Amedeo Porro Arte Moderna
e Contemporanea; London, Ben Brown Fine Arts,
Lucio Fontana, Sedici Sculture/Sixteen Sculptures, 1937-1967, 2007-2008, pp. 90-91, no. 7
London, Ben Brown Fine Arts and Amedeo Porro
Arte Moderna e Contemporanea, *From De Chirico to Cattelan: A Survey of 20th Century Italian Art*,
8 October - 30 November 2012, p. 18

Bibliography
E. Crispolti, *Lucio Fontana, Catalogo Ragionato di Sculture, Dipinti, Ambientazioni*, Edizioni Skira,
Milan 2006, vol. I, p. 307, no. 54 SC 10

The production of "spatial sculptures", terracotta tablets which were barely marked by splashes of paint applied after firing and which were always perforated and usually rectangular in shape, dates back to the early 1950s, but it intensifies in 1954. It is likely that the series of *Concetti spaziali* on ceramic tablets made that year – the number about thirty in all – was directly related to the international event and made before and immediately after it. It also may have stemmed from the urgency to participate in the avant-garde spirit with a work that was aligned with the contemporary production of perforated "spatial concepts" on canvas, further exploring this approach. While the artist was making a series of stones in which fragments of coloured glass stuck to the canvas represent the bright, protruding element that communicates with the perforations, the composition of the tablets reflected the search for even greater simplicity, as in the work *Concetto spaziale* (1954). In this piece, in which the terracotta is painted matt black with white drops of enamel, the parallel rows of perforations (of different diameters), marked out on the monochrome space as though along diagonals, are only partly highlighted by the overlapping drips.
The bright part is therefore obtained by the single drop of paints which maintains an inner expressive charge. In this case there is a simple black/white two tone although other plans for the same series involved splashes of different colours, only circumscribed to the holes, capable of contrasting the empty space expressed by the perforations. Using this expedient based on both simplicity but also a certain playfulness, Fontana once more created a subtle alternative to the chromatic exasperation of Jorn or Appel's ceramics which where always rather confused with garish colours and intentionally plastic. Instead he emphasised the need of a calmer, broader spatial imagination which would subsequently find a more complete expression in the cycle of "plaster casts" and "inks".

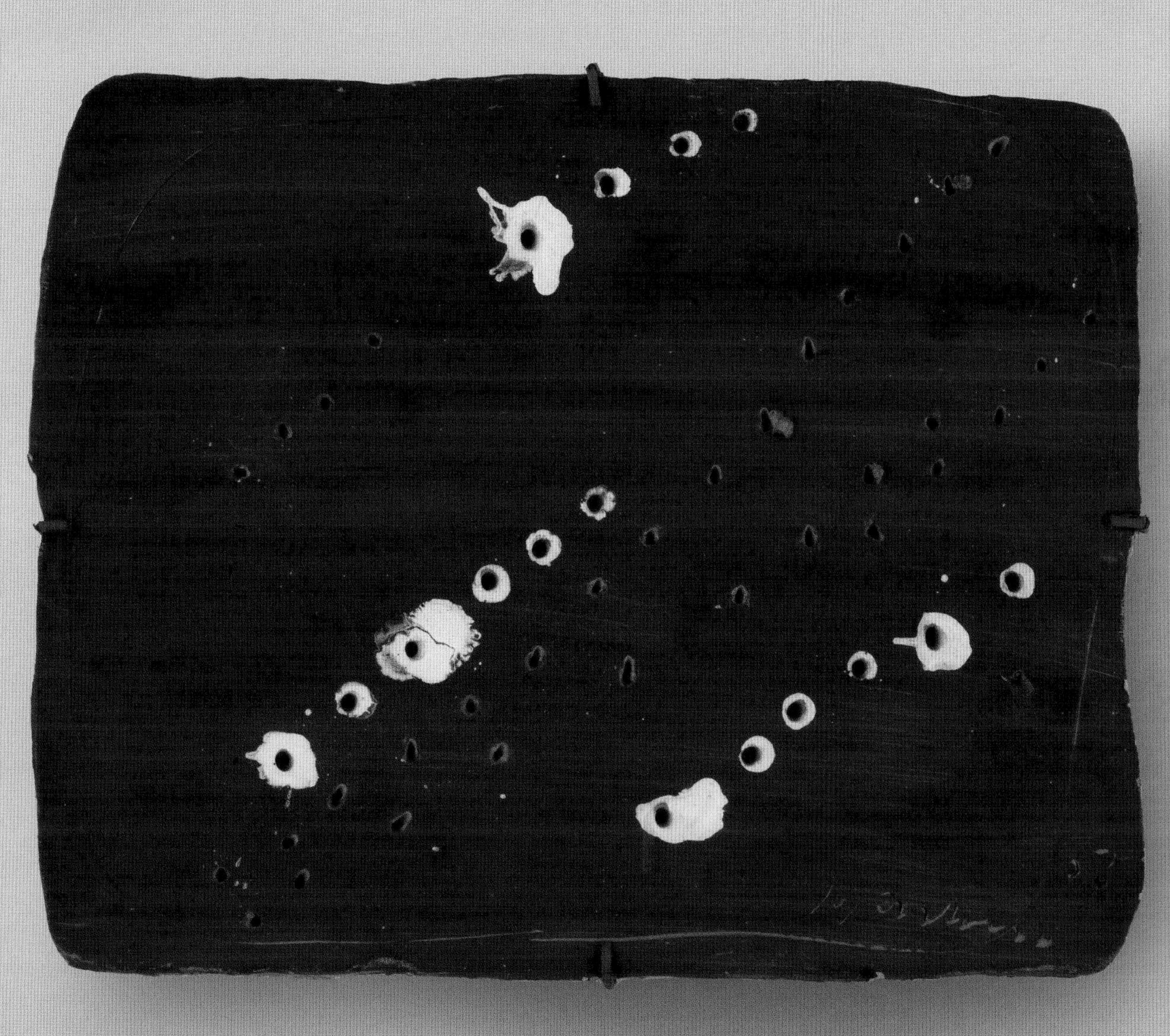

CONCETTO SPAZIALE
[SPATIAL CONCEPT], 1955

Signed and dated *l. fontana 55* on the lower right
Oil, waterpaint and stones on canvas
50 x 40 cm. (19 3/4 x 15 3/4 in.)

Provenance
Private collection, Rome

This work is registered in the *Archivio della Fondazione Lucio Fontana, Milan* under number 2838/1.

In 1955, while busily working on ceramics for the preparation of three exhibitions – one of which is the well-known one at the San Fedele Gallery in Milan, devoted to sacred art only – in the studio of Corso Monforte 23, the artist developed his *pietre* (stones) series, a remarkable set of *Concetti spaziali* (Spatial concepts) featuring the use of coloured glass pieces glued on canvas and then painted. Five *Concetti spaziali* of this series were displayed at the Rome Quadriennale in 1955, representing the most evident expression of the series and its first diffusion outside the specialised field.
The *Concetto spaziale* (1955) shows a formal motif at its centre, a mass of matter obtained by using a set of glass pieces glued on the canvas, all of which are painted with the same tone of grey as the background and matted by abundant paint. Its star-shaped and arch-shaped arrangement reaches out in five directions with some trails of vitreous materials. However, the galactic motif is crossed by two sequences of glossy glass elements, a white trail of light going from one side of the painting to the other, and a vertical trail of darker glass. This shape forms a counterpoint with a number of punctures of different sizes, showing a star-shaped or round section and following a curving, merry line that reflects the moving paths suggested by the element at the centre. The grey surface of the canvas calls to mind the celestial vault, where the cosmic appearance takes place, but it is also the space of mutual penetration between matter and antimatter, between the dark physicality of a raw material and the brightness of some of the paths, between a surface that is still tangible and harmonious arrangements of holes suggesting the infinite space.
Fontana's detail features the construction of a shape, though imagined, yet still recognisable, highlighted by the development of holes. The romantic feeling created by the distribution of the drawing on the painting's surface and the expressionist dramatization of the gesture give way to a placid structure that is pure spatial evocation.

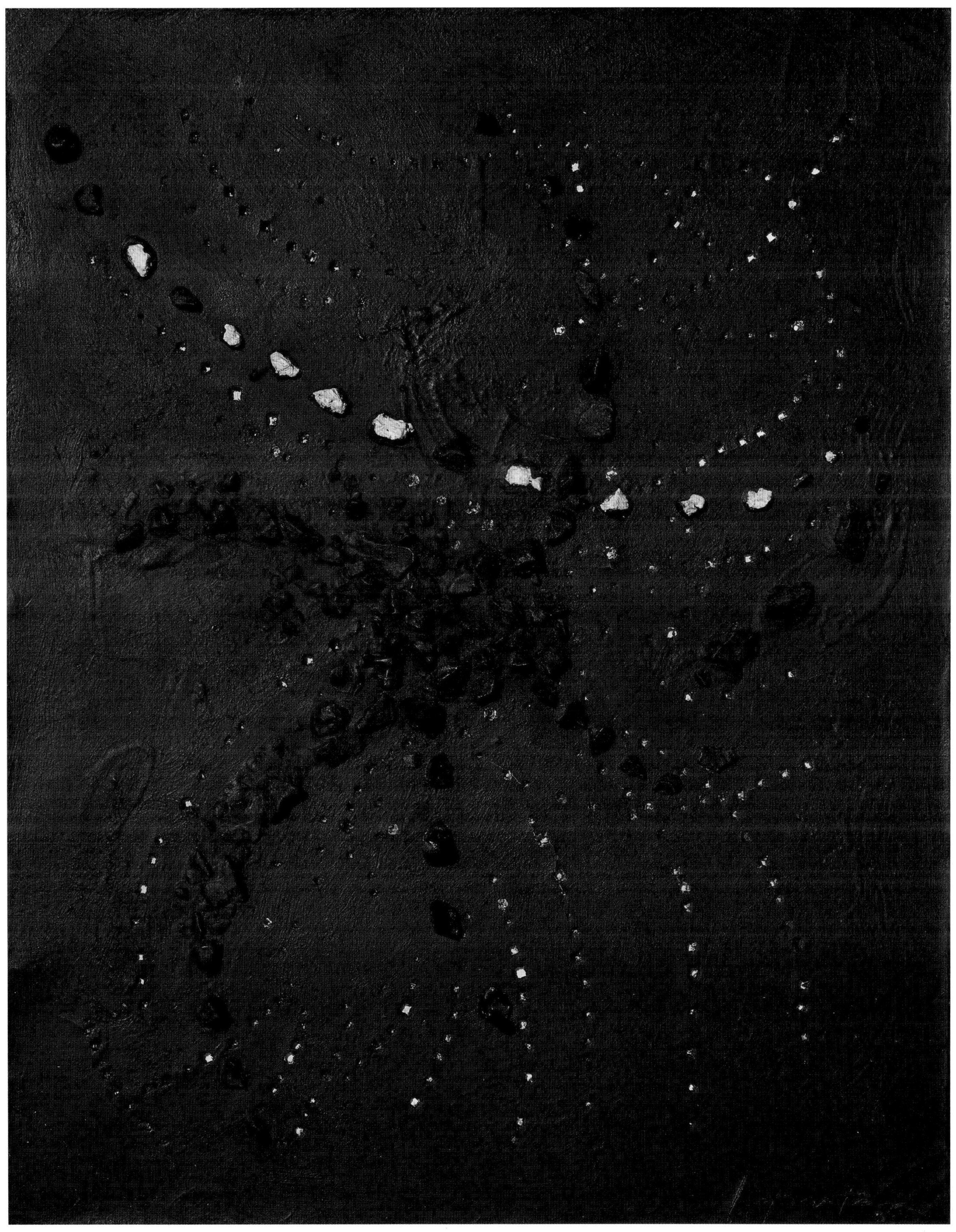

CONCETTO SPAZIALE [SPATIAL CONCEPT], 1956

Signed and dated *l. Fontana 56* on the lower right; signed, titled, dated and inscribed *N. 90 / "Concetto spaziale" / l. fontana / 56* on the reverse
Oil, mixed media and glitter on canvas
134.5 × 100 cm. (53 × 39 3/8 in.)

Provenance
Marisa del Re Gallery, New York; Private collection, Milan; Galleria Blu, Milan; Private collection, Milan; Studio Casoli, Milan; Private collection, Milan; Private collection, Milan; Fabian Carlsson Gallery, London

Exhibitions
London, Fabian Carlsson Gallery, 1989
Venice, *La Biennale di Venezia, LXV Esposizione Internazionale d'Arte*, 11 June - 15 October 1993, vol. I, p. 390

Bibliography
Giampaolo, *Fontana*, in "Rossana", a. III, no. 2, Milan 1960, February, pp. 116-117
E. Crispolti, *Lucio Fontana, Catalogue Raisonné des Peintures, Sculptures et Environnements Spatiaux*, Edition La Connaissance, Brussels 1974, vol. II, pp. 50-51, no. 56 BA 31
E. Crispolti, *Lucio Fontana, Catalogo Generale*, Edizioni Electa, Milan 1986, vol. I, p. 174, no. 56 BA 31
E. Crispolti, *Lucio Fontana, Catalogo Ragionato di Sculture, Dipinti, Ambientazioni*, Edizioni Skira, Milan 2006, vol. I, p. 327, no. 56 BA 31, pl. CXLIX, illustrated in colour

Some of the 'baroque' *Concetti spaziali* (Spatial concepts) from 1956 display a recognisable relief image, a large face or stylised figurative element in the painted space, rather than an invented shape only.

However, in *Concetto spaziale*, 1956, an abstract, white, irregular geometric perimeter, whose vague outline was applied by trowel, calls to mind an architectural layout and includes a number of geometrising subdivisions and spaces, a far-off memory of Paul Klee's lines. This is a structure that floats in the red space from which, along the perimeter, organic-shaped elements – sort of peduncles – develop, in the corners and in the upper part of the painting. Here, namely in the top right, the artist would seem to suggest the stylised head of a howling animal. It is a scenic representation, showing surreal and imaginary features, which takes place within the wider red-painted background. Inside the white structure, between the individual subdivisions, the thick layer of multi-material pastes – such as sand, impasto, glue and glitter – illustrates the reference to Baroque that Enrico Crispolti himself, by looking at this series of paintings back in 1959, identified as one of the permanent features of his master's work. The holes follow straight and slanting paths, and it would almost seem as if those paths relied on the central shape, just like a corollary that, however, identifies a further spatial plane in the different shades of reds setting this appearance in a borderless space. In *Concetto spaziale*, 1956, the contrast between the memory of a shape, the notion of an image and the inability to bring the scene back to an immediately intelligible human scale is more evident, as the artist leaves the function of suggesting a fantastic, imaginary vision of pure seduction to the chromatic combinations and to the seduction of colour pastes. In depicting an event, Fontana even questions our relationship with the scene, in the belief that events in the cosmic space occur according to categories that are not linked to mere mathematic formulas.

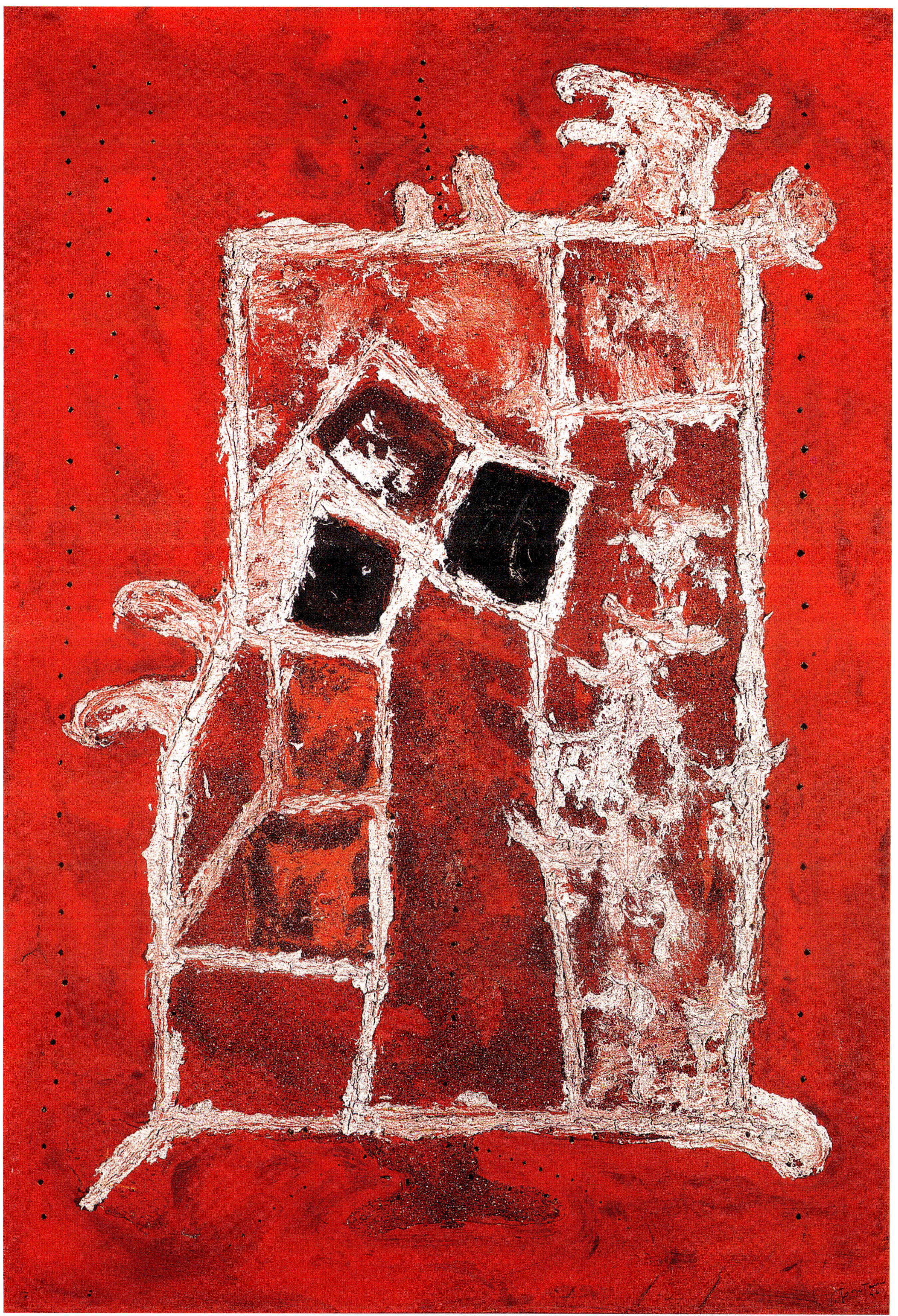

CONCETTO SPAZIALE
[SPATIAL CONCEPT], 1955-60

Incised with signature *l. fontana*
Painted terracotta
20 × 25.5 × 18.6 cm. (7 7/8 × 10 1/8 × 7 3/8 in.)

Provenance
Galerie di Meo, Paris

This work is registered in the *Archivio della Fondazione Lucio Fontana, Milan* under number 2368/1.

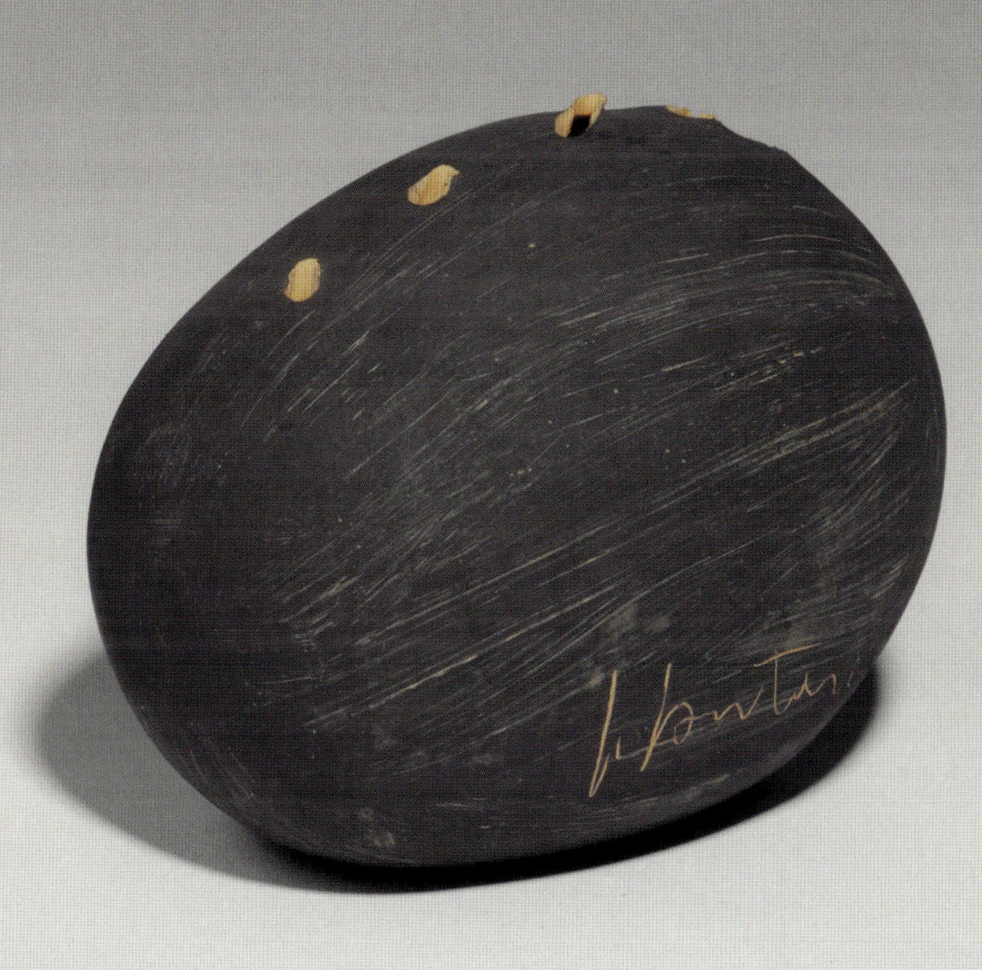

CONCETTO SPAZIALE [SPATIAL CONCEPT], 1957

Signed and dated *l. fontana / 57* on the reverse
Pastels and collage on canvas
100 × 70 cm. (39 3/8 × 27 1/2 in.)

Provenance
Galleria Blu, Milan; Private collection, Milan; Private collection, Cologne

Exhibitions
Milan, Galleria Blu, *Fontana*, 5 October - 5 November 1964, no. 28
Milan, Palazzo Reale, *Lucio Fontana*, 19 April - 21 June 1972, p. 163, no. 118
Milan, Palazzo Reale, *Anni Cinquanta. La Nascita della Creatività Italiana*, 4 March - 3 July 2005, p. 433

Bibliography
E. Crispolti, *Lucio Fontana, Catalogue Raisonné des Peintures, Sculptures et Environnements Spatiaux*, Brussels 1974, vol. II, pp. 56-57, no. 57 G 20
E. Crispolti, *Lucio Fontana, Catalogo Generale*, Milan 1986, vol. I, p. 196
R. Pasini, *L'Informale. Stati Uniti – Europa – Italia*, Bologna 1995, no. 103
E. Crispolti, *Lucio Fontana, Catalogo Ragionato di Sculture, Dipinti, Ambientazioni*, Milan 2006, vol. I, p. 351, no. 57 G 20

In the *gessi* (impastos) series, developed since 1954, Fontana uses impastos of pastel paints to express a new lay-down of colour-surface and a peculiar plaster-like – or 'wall-like' – effect. Still in 1957, he alternated a baroque material texture with an appreciation for simple surface, of tonal nature, where the presence of nuclear or rising shapes is predominant. The artist ironically called his paintings with arched shapes '*panettoni*', and those with circular elements 'walls'.

Concetto spaziale (Spatial concept), 1957, belongs to the category of 'walls' and features a blue shape in the middle, neither a circle, nor a nucleus, which consists of a scrap of cut-out canvas glued on the surface. In this way, the artist achieves the desired effect of an elusive element, due both to its unique shape and impalpable volumetric texture, which of course becomes predominant over the grey background. In 1993, Jole de Sanna construed the *gessi* series in relation to a never-extinguished naturalistic approach: "the powders, the embryos, the glutens enrich the path with natural references."[1] In fact, the series is linked to the artist's 1931 coloured plaster and scratched panels, from which the overall plaster-like and impasto-like effect is taken up. Since 1954, when they were displayed at the Venice Biennale together with the artist's latest spatial experiences, Fontana's attention towards these first instances of abstract art – which also consisted in the physical remake of some works destroyed by the time – aimed at seizing the essence and translating it into a new dimension. Namely, a vague suggestion of the 1930s' experience remains in this example, while a new sensitivity arises: the suspension effect of shape in space and a hint of lyricism in the sequences of holes contribute to the meaning of appearance of a shape. The study of a simple, elementary element, whose dimensions are yet ambiguous and elusive, in relief against the background, places Fontana far in advance of the American reflections on 'primary structures'.

[1] J. De Sanna, *Lucio Fontana, materia, spazio, concetto*, Mursia, 1993, p 113.

GUERRIERI [WARRIORS], 1957

Incised with signature and date *l. fontana 57* along the edge
Painted terracotta
47 × 47 cm. (18 1/2 × 18 1/2 in.)

Provenance
Galleria Marconi, Milan

This work is registered in the *Archivio della Fondazione Lucio Fontana, Milan* under number *1900/257*.

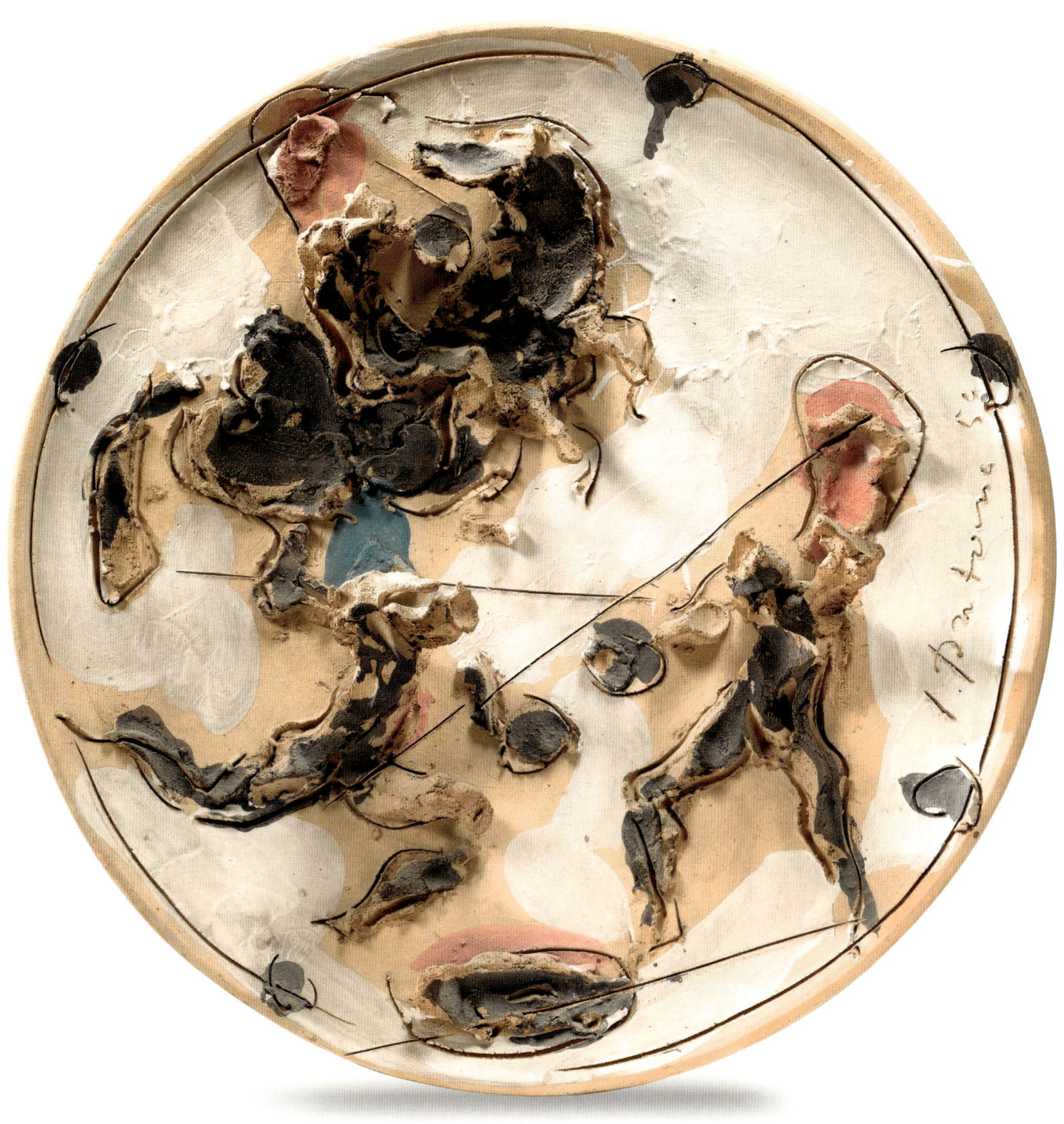

CONCETTO SPAZIALE [SPATIAL CONCEPT], 1958

Signed, titled and dated *l.Fontana / Concetto spaziale / 1958* on the reverse
Incisions on paper canvas
97 × 130 cm. (38 1/4 × 51 1/8 in.)

Provenance
T.R.F. Collection, Milan; Nahmad Collection, Geneva

Exhibitions
Turin, Galleria Civica d'Arte Moderna, *Lucio Fontana*, 5 February - 28 March 1970, no. 174, pl. 164
London, Estorick Collection of Modern Italian Art, *Lucio Fontana: At the Roots of Spatialism,* 27 June - 9 September 2007
Milan, Amedeo Porro Arte Moderna e Contemporanea; London, Ben Brown Fine Arts, *Lucio Fontana, Sedici Sculture/Sixteen Sculptures, 1937 - 1967*, 2007-2008, pp. 8-9
New York, Sperone Westwater, *ZERO in New York*, 6 November - 20 December 2008, p. 224, illustrated in colour
London, Ben Brown Fine Arts, *Heinz Mack / Lucio Fontana*, 6 October - 21 December 2010, p. 45
London, Ben Brown Fine Arts and Amedeo Porro Arte Moderna e Contemporanea, *From De Chirico to Cattelan: A Survey of 20th Century Italian Art,* 8 October - 30 November 2012, p. 21

Bibliography
Vernissage, Kunst bis aufs Messer: Lucio Fontana, March 1960, no. 2
E. Crispolti, *Lucio Fontana, Catalogue Raisonné des Peintures, Sculptures et Environnements Spatiaux,* Edition La Connaissance, Brussels 1974, vol. II, p. 76 - 77, no. 58 CA 2
E. Crispolti, *Lucio Fontana, Catalogo Generale,* Edizioni Electa, Milan 1986, vol. I, p. 267, no. 58 CA 2
E. Crispolti, *Lucio Fontana, Catalogo Ragionato di Sculture, Dipinti, Ambientazioni*, Edizioni Skira, Milan 2006, vol. I, p. 434, no. 58 CA 2

On 16th February 1957, Lucio Fontana, after the opening of his personal exhibition at the Galleria del Naviglio, where he mostly displayed *pietre* (stones) and *barocchi* (baroques), confided in his friend Mario Bardini, "as usual after every exhibition, the period of crisis, glitter or no glitter? Painter or sculptor? Spatial or realist? And so time goes by in my everlasting and content illusion!" Within his creative universe, the time was about to come – and he knew it – for the settling of his painting towards a debate on surface and a clearer tonal formulation. On the other hand, during 1958, his contacts with young representatives of a new sensitivity increased, especially with Piero Manzoni. Over the year, a real friendship arose and grew stronger between Fontana and Manzoni: the older artist promoted and was pleased to witness the creation of Manzoni's first *Achromes*, of which he appreciated the new and clear objectification of the 'tabula rasa'. Maybe influenced by this new Milanese atmosphere – which would lead, in 1959, to re-publish Guido Ballo's paper written for Fontana's room at the 1959 Biennale with the title *Oltre la pittura* (Beyond painting) in the first issue of Azimuth – by the end of the year the artist had acquired further awareness of the need for resetting, one of the pillars of his poetics.
Fontana started back from zero, from the paper sheet and a repeated gesture.
The *carte* (papers) series is formed by 50 documented works in total, and especially the rare set of three or four museum works – to which *Concetto spaziale* (Spatial concept), 1958 belongs – witnesses his new start. The surface of the painting is made stiff by glued paper and becomes the 'field' for an action provided with its own specific grammar of signs and high metaphorical content: the small cut, the slash is arranged to draw a rhythmic sequence. It seems like the artist, over this brief series of *carte* on canvas, has tried the new slash gesture, which he had already tested in 1957 on the spatial ceilings of Procchio and in the Altimani wall graffiti in Milan, though with a new meaning. The slash here is no longer associated with any sign other than itself, and in the repeated consequentiality it creates a trace, a wave movement, disclosing the very process that generated it. Not only the slash opens to the infinite; it becomes the metaphor for the artist's repeated and irreversible action itself.

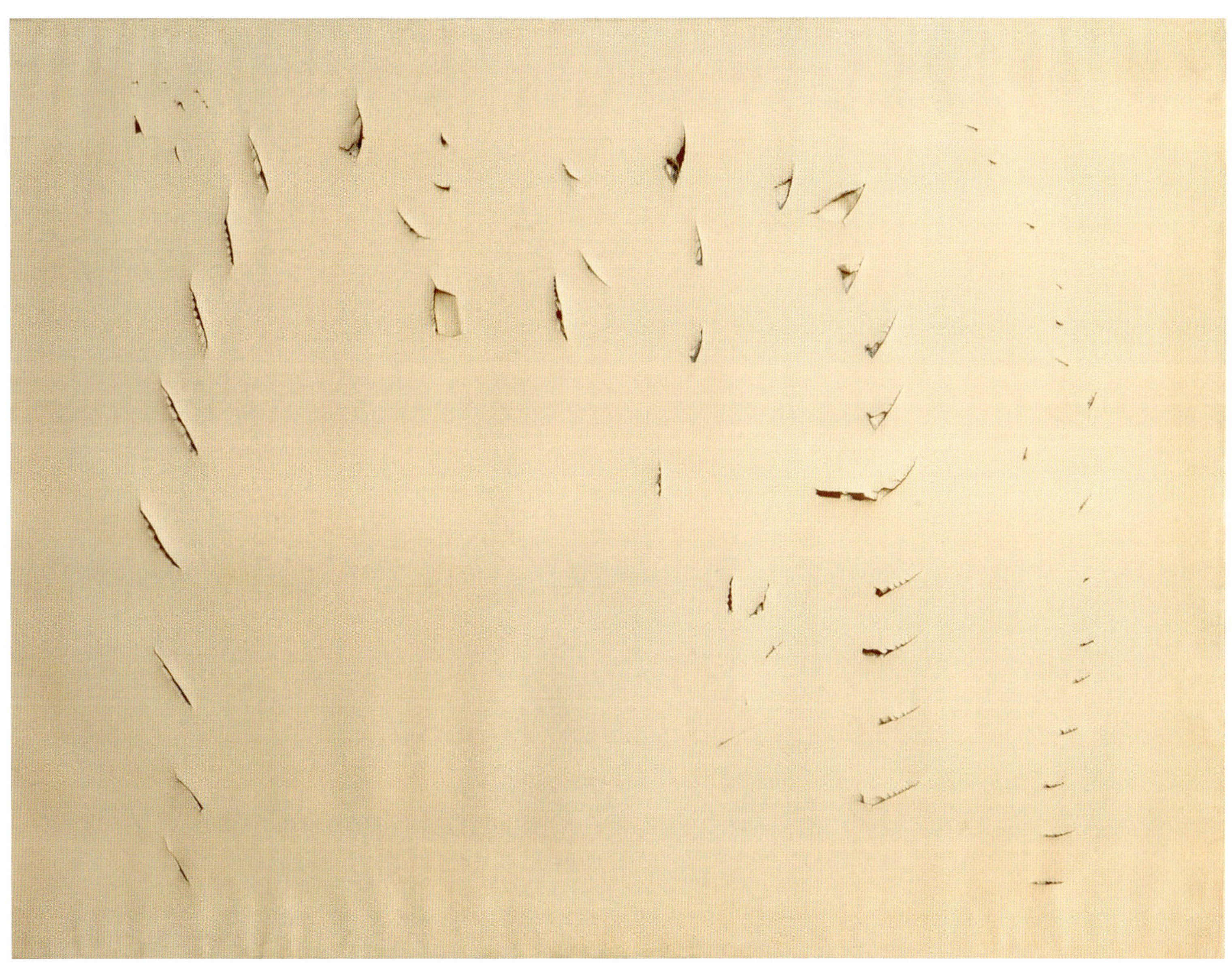

CONCETTO SPAZIALE
[SPATIAL CONCEPT], 1958

Signed, titled and dated *L. Fontana / Concetto Spaziale / 1958* on the reverse
Aniline, pencil and collage on canvas
130 × 97 cm. (51 1/8 × 38 1/4 in.)

Provenance
Galleria Marlborough, Rome; Cattaneo Collection, Brescia; Private collection, Monza; Private collection, Milan; Private collection, Hamburg

Exhibitions
L`Aquila, Castello Cinquecentesco, *Aspetti dell'Arte Contemporanea: Omaggio a Cagli, Omaggio a Fontana, Omaggio a Quaroni - Retrospettive Archeologiche,* 28 July - 6 October 1963, no. 140
Buenos Aires, Centro de Artes Visuales del Instituto Torcuato di Tella, *Lucio Fontana*, 26 July - 28 August 1966, no. 16
Minneapolis, Walker Art Center; Austin, University of Texas Art Museum, *Lucio Fontana, The Spatial Concept of Art*, 6 January - 13 February 1966, no. 18
Amsterdam, Stedelijk Museum; Eindhoven, Stedelijk van Abbemuseum, *Lucio Fontana - Concetti Spaziali*, 1967, no. 22
Humlebaek, Louisiana Museum, *Fontana*, January - February 1967, no. 22
Stockholm, Moderna Museet, *Fontana, Idéer om Rymden*, 26 August - 1 October 1967, no. 22
Hanover, Kestner - Gesellschaft, *Lucio Fontana*, 25 January - 25 February 1968, no. 22
Zurich, de Pury & Luxembourg, *Lucio Fontana*, 10 October - 6 December 2002, no. 70
New York, Gagosian Gallery, *Lucio Fontana. Ambienti Spaziali*, 3 May - 30 June 2012, p. 239, no. 260
London, Ben Brown Fine Arts and Amedeo Porro Arte Moderna e Contemporanea, *From De Chirico to Cattelan: A Survey of 20th Century Italian Art*, 8 October - 30 November 2012, p. 25

Bibliography
E. Crispolti, *Omaggio a Fontana*, Beniamino Carucci Editore, Assisi - Rome 1971, p. 162, no. 170
E. Crispolti, *Lucio Fontana, Catalogue Raisonné des Peintures, Sculptures et Environnements Spatiaux*, Edition La Connaissance, Brussels 1974, vol. II, p. 63, no. 58 I 36
E. Crispolti, *Lucio Fontana, Catalogo Generale*, Edizioni Electa, Milan 1986, vol. I, p. 218, no. 58 I 36
E. Crispolti, *Lucio Fontana, Catalogo Ragionato di Sculture, Dipinti, Ambientazioni*, Edizioni Skira, Milan 2006, vol. I, p. 377, no. 58 I 36

"When he realises he has achieved full control over matter, he has exploited the most unpredictable and evocative effects, he castigates matter itself, even further reduces his style to the most essential means (...) everything in Fontana's recent spatial compositions is reduced to the most elementary and simple means: this is very clearly put into effect in the urgency of his voice, which is a unique artist's voice." With these words, Guido Ballo introduced the new *inchiostri* (inks) series at the Biennale in 1958; these works featured the use of anilines, often on canvases mounted on the reverse side to exploit the raw side, and characterised by a fluctuating imagination, also known as 'cloudlike'.
In *Concetto spaziale* (Spatial concept), 1958, the distinctive value of few, essential tones provides an atmosphere that does not refer to any image, neither to portions of objects, nor to blurry visions. These are mere transparencies that the lightness of anilines suggests could refer to a portion of a landscape, while not ensuring any presence at all. In the central position, a single element floats, a small cut-out canvas, punctured by two lines of almost invisible holes. The shape emerges and is slightly in relief against the background, with an ambiguous game of spaces that seem to find their natural harmony while influencing and overlapping each other. The value of energy and light conveyed by colour, which is predominant in this painting, is not jeopardised by the only presence which, in fact, provides a small fragment of humanity and existence, almost as the last witness to a human reaction to the loss of all space-time references.
Since the early 1960s, this *Concetto spaziale* dated 1958 has been considered a classic example of this creative phase of the artist and was displayed at Fontana's first important retrospective exhibition, curated by Enrico Crispolti, in the Castello Cinquecentesco of L'Aquila in 1963.

CONCETTO SPAZIALE
[SPATIAL CONCEPT], 1958

Incised with signature and date *l. fontana 58* along the lower edge
Painted terracotta
25 × 17.2 × 17.2 cm. (9 7/8 × 6 3/4 × 6 3/4 in.)

Provenance
Acquired directly from the artist by the family of the previous owner

This work is registered in the *Archivio della Fondazione Lucio Fontana, Milan* under number 1737/104

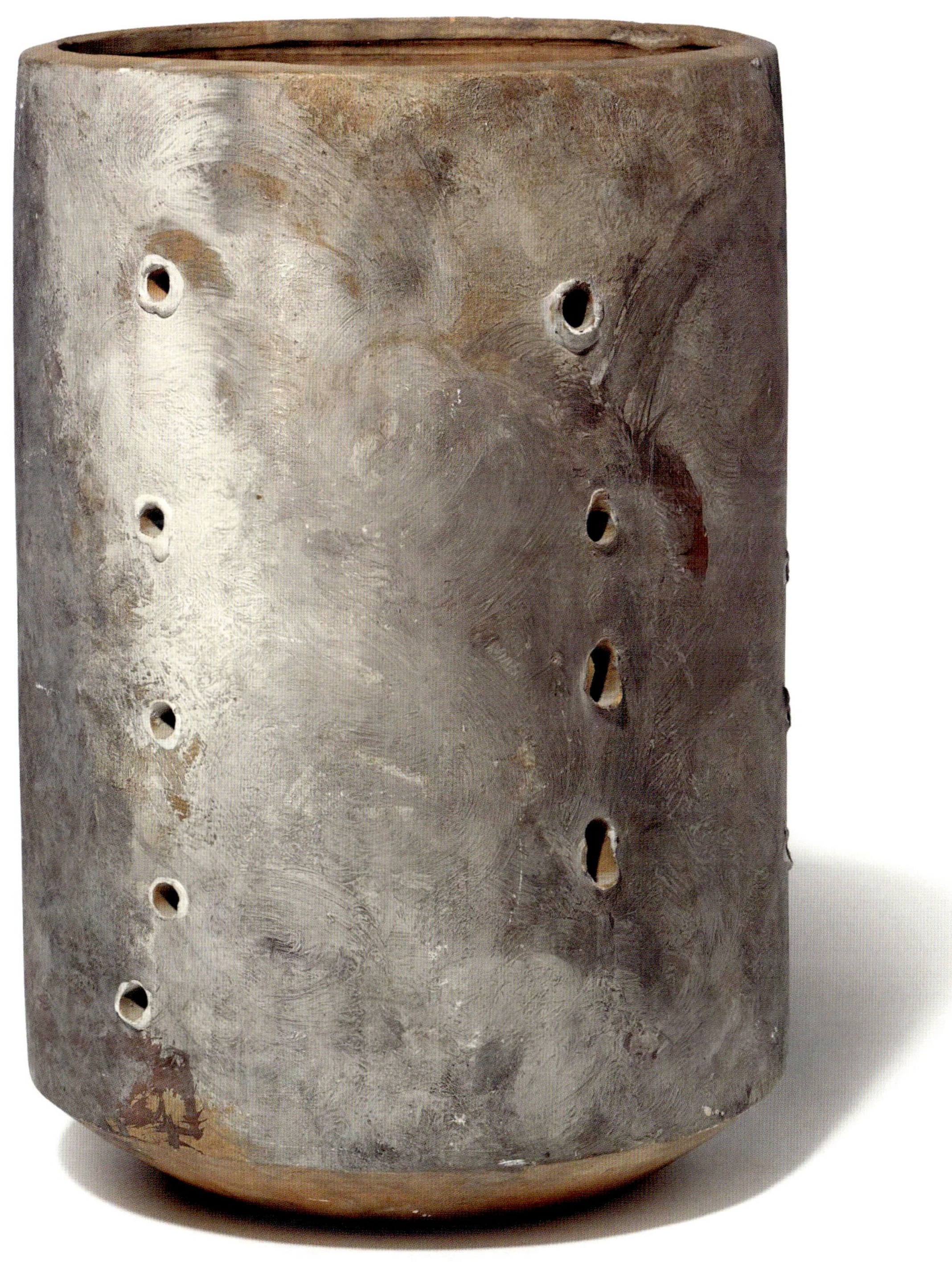

DEPOSIZIONE DALLA CROCE [DEPOSITION FROM THE CROSS], 1959-60

Incised with signature *l. fontana* on the lower left
Glazed ceramic
53 × 35 cm. (20 7/8 × 13 3/4 in.)

Provenance
E. Cattaneo collection, Milan

This work is registered in the *Archivio della Fondazione Lucio Fontana, Milan* under number 386/2.

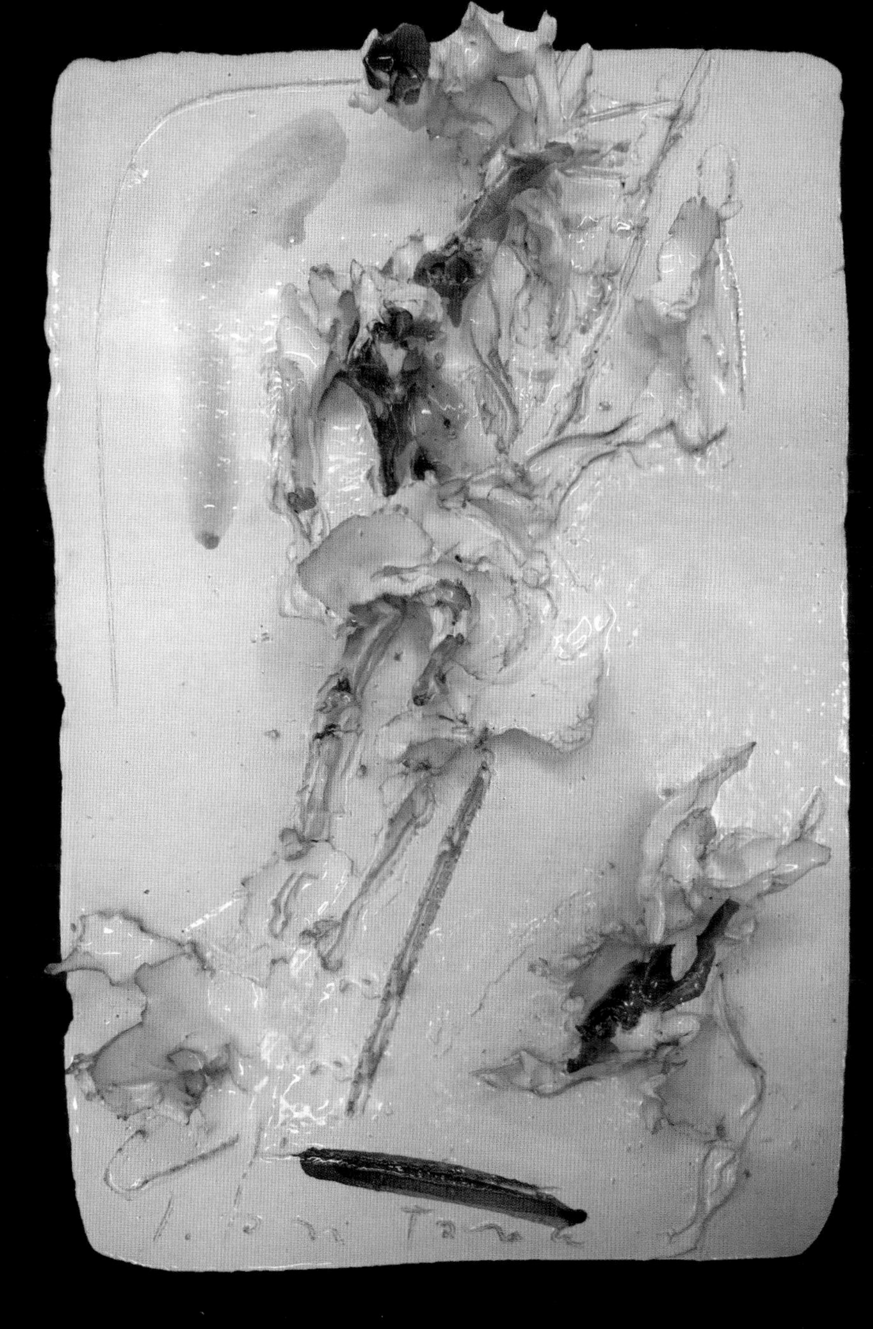

CONCETTO SPAZIALE
[SPATIAL CONCEPT], 1961

Signed *l. Fontana* on the lower right
Oil on canvas
80 × 100 cm. (31 1/2 × 39 3/8 in.)

Provenance
Galerie Schmela, Dusseldorf; Galerie Gunar, Düsseldorf; Private collection, Milan

Exhibitions
Milan, Galleria Civica d'Arte Moderna; Rome, Palazzo delle Esposizioni, *Mostra della Critica Italiana 1961*, 13 February - 11 March 1961, p. 40, no. 44
Wuppertal, Kunst- und Museumsverein, *Hommage à Fontana*, 20 September - 2 November 1969, no. 25
London, Ben Brown Fine Arts, *Heinz Mack / Lucio Fontana*, 6 October - 21 December 2010, pp. 48-51
London, Ben Brown Fine Arts and Amedeo Porro Arte Moderna e Contemporanea, *From De Chirico to Cattelan: A Survey of 20th Century Italian Art*, 8 October - 30 November 2012, p. 22

Bibliography
E. Crispolti, *Lucio Fontana, Catalogue Raisonné des Peintures, Sculptures et Environnements Spatiaux*, Edition La Connaissance, Brussels 1974, vol. II, p. 112, no. 61 O 65
E. Crispolti, *Lucio Fontana, Catalogo Generale*, Edizioni Electa, Milan 1986, vol. I, p. 376, no. 61 O 65
AA.VV. *Arte all'incanto*, Edizioni Longanesi & co., Milan 1987, p. 240
E. Crispolti, *Lucio Fontana, Catalogo Ragionato di Sculture, Dipinti, Ambientazioni*, Edizioni Skira, Milan 2006, vol. II, p. 564, no. 61 O 65

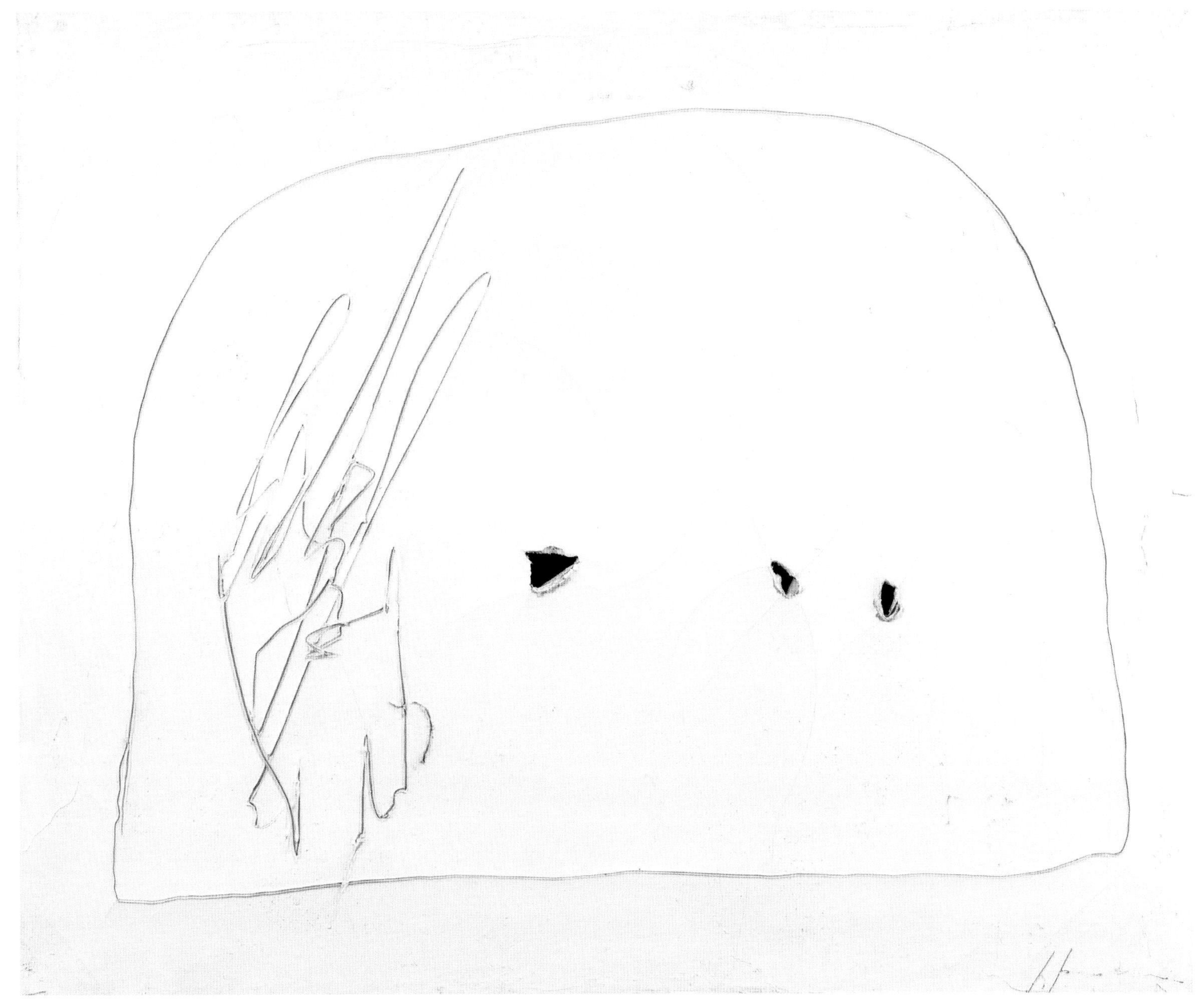

CONCETTO SPAZIALE [SPATIAL CONCEPT], 1962-64

Incised with signature *l. Fontana* on the underside
Glazed ceramic
27,8 × 22,5 × 23,5 cm. (10 × 11 1/2 × 8 1/2 in.)

Provenance
Jan and Ingeborg van der Marck, West Lebanon, New Hampshire; Vidal Sassoon, Los Angeles

Exhibitions
Zurich, Gimpel & Hanover, *Lucio Fontana Peinture, Sculpture,* 21 May -15 June 1963
Minneapolis, Minneapolis Walker Art Center; Austin, University of Texas Art Museum, *Lucio Fontana. The Spatial Concept of Art,* 6 January – 13 February 1966, p. 13, no. 50
New York, the Solomon R. Guggenheim Museum, *Lucio Fontana 1899 - 1968, A Retrospective,* 20 October - 11 December 1977, p. 101, no. 97
New York, Marisa del Re Gallery, *Lucio Fontana Conquest of Space,* November - December 1986
Milan, Amedeo Porro Arte Moderna e Contemporanea; London, Ben Brown Fine Arts, *Lucio Fontana, Sedici Sculture/Sixteen Sculptures, 1937 - 1967,* 2007 - 2008, pp. 104-105, no. 14
London, Ben Brown Fine Arts and Amedeo Porro Arte Moderna e Contemporanea, *From De Chirico to Cattelan: A Survey of 20th Century Italian Art,* 8 October - 30 November 2012, p. 26

Bibliography
P. Rouve, *Lucio Fontana,* in "Quadrum", Brussels 1963, no. 14, p. 53

This work is registered in the *Archivio della Fondazione Lucio Fontana, Milan* under number 3329/23.

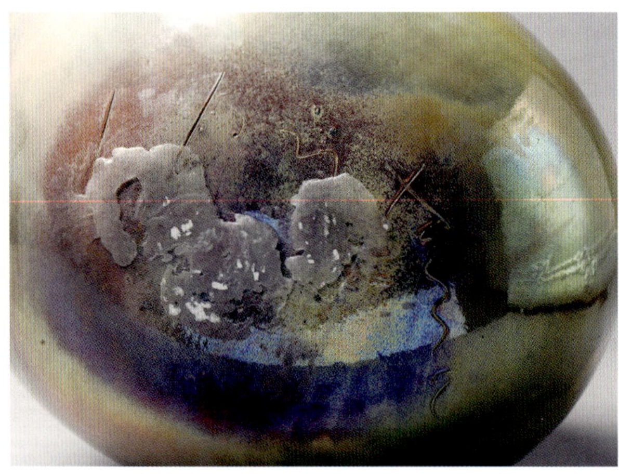

Concetto spaziale, 1962-64, detail

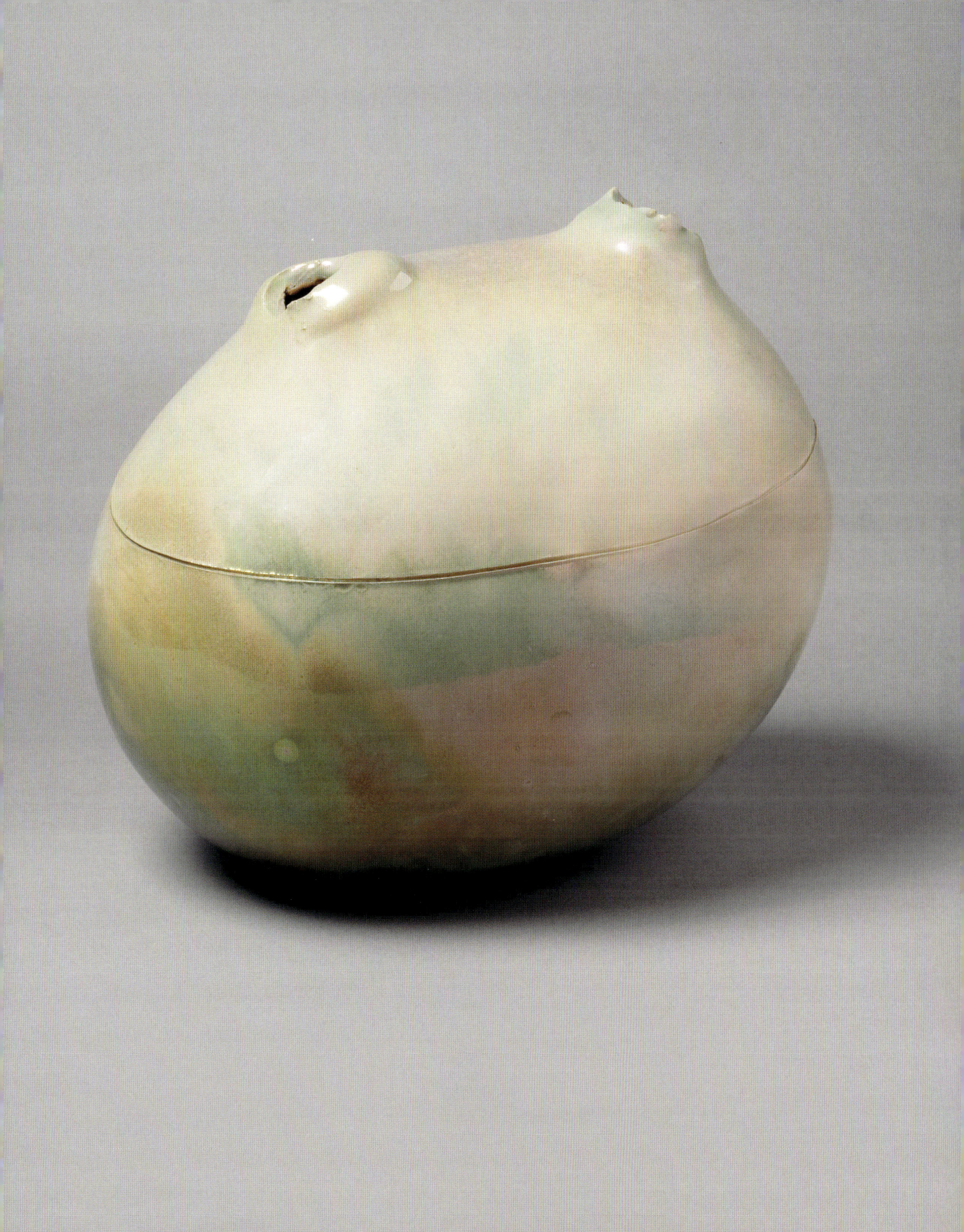

CONCETTO SPAZIALE
[SPATIAL CONCEPT], 1960-1965

Signed *l. Fontana* on the lower right
Painted terracotta
26.5 × 41.5 × 5 cm. (10 3/8 × 16 3/8 × 2 in.)

Provenance
Galerie Toni Gerber, Bern; Private collection, Germany

Exhibitions
London, Ben Brown Fine Arts and Amedeo Porro Arte Moderna e Contemporanea, *From De Chirico to Cattelan: A Survey of 20th Century Italian Art,* 8 October - 30 November 2012, p. 19

This work is registered in the *Archivio della Fondazione Lucio Fontana, Milan* under number *2678/1.*

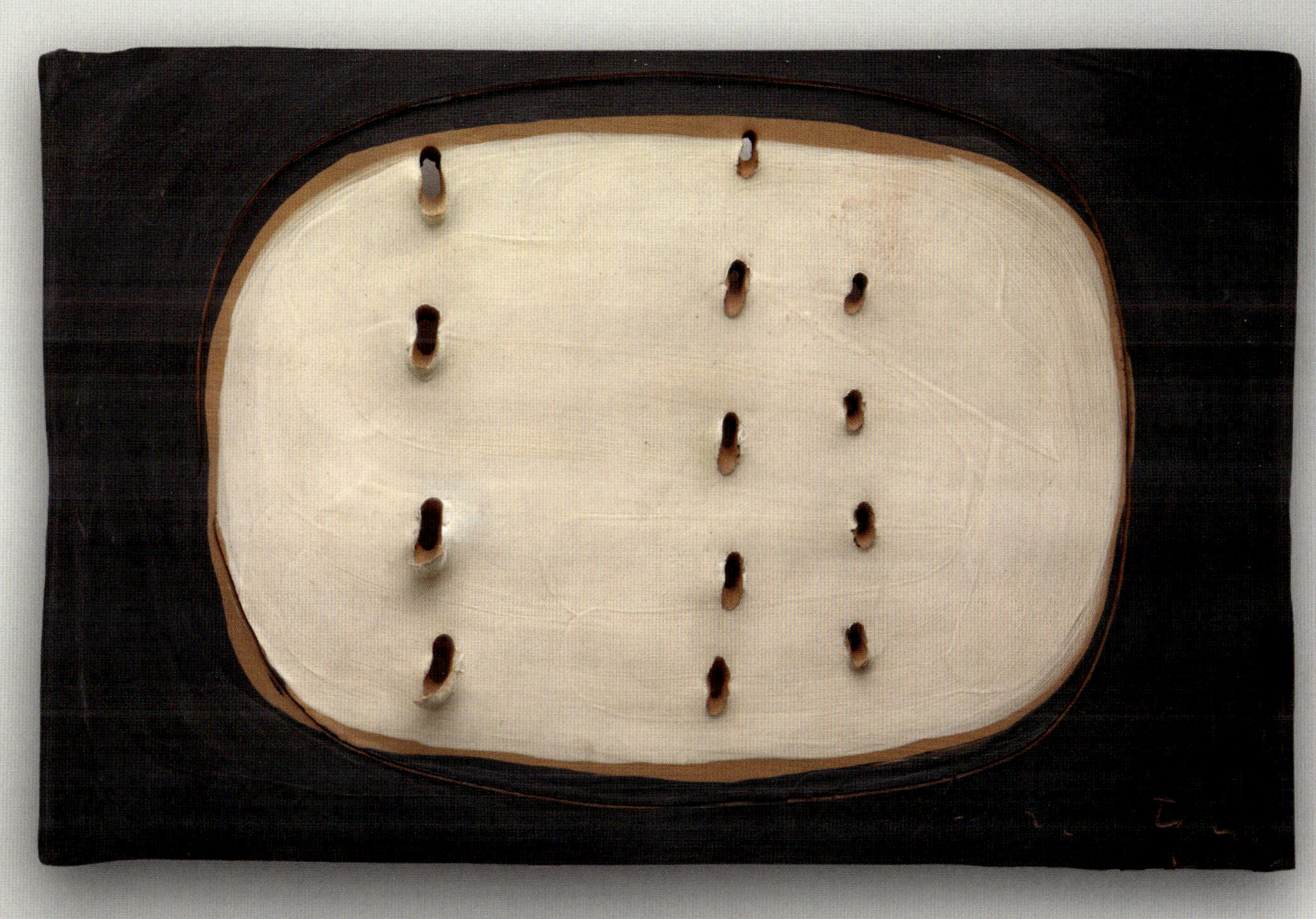

CONCETTO SPAZIALE
[SPATIAL CONCEPT], 1957

Signed and dated *fontana 57* on the lower right
Ink on paper
25.9 × 20.2 cm. (10 1/4 × 8 in.)

Provenance
Gift from the artist
Francesco de Bartolomeis, Turin; Private collection, Turin

Exhibitions
London, Ben Brown Fine Arts, *Lucio Fontana - Paintings, Sculptures and Drawings*, 5 February - 20 May 2005, p. 75

Bibliography
L. M. Barbero, *Lucio Fontana. Catalogo Ragionato dei Disegni e delle Carte*, Edizioni Skira, Milano 2013, vol. I, p. 106; vol. III, p. 759, n. 57 DSP 50

This work is registered in the *Archivio della Fondazione Lucio Fontana, Milan* under number 3329/16.

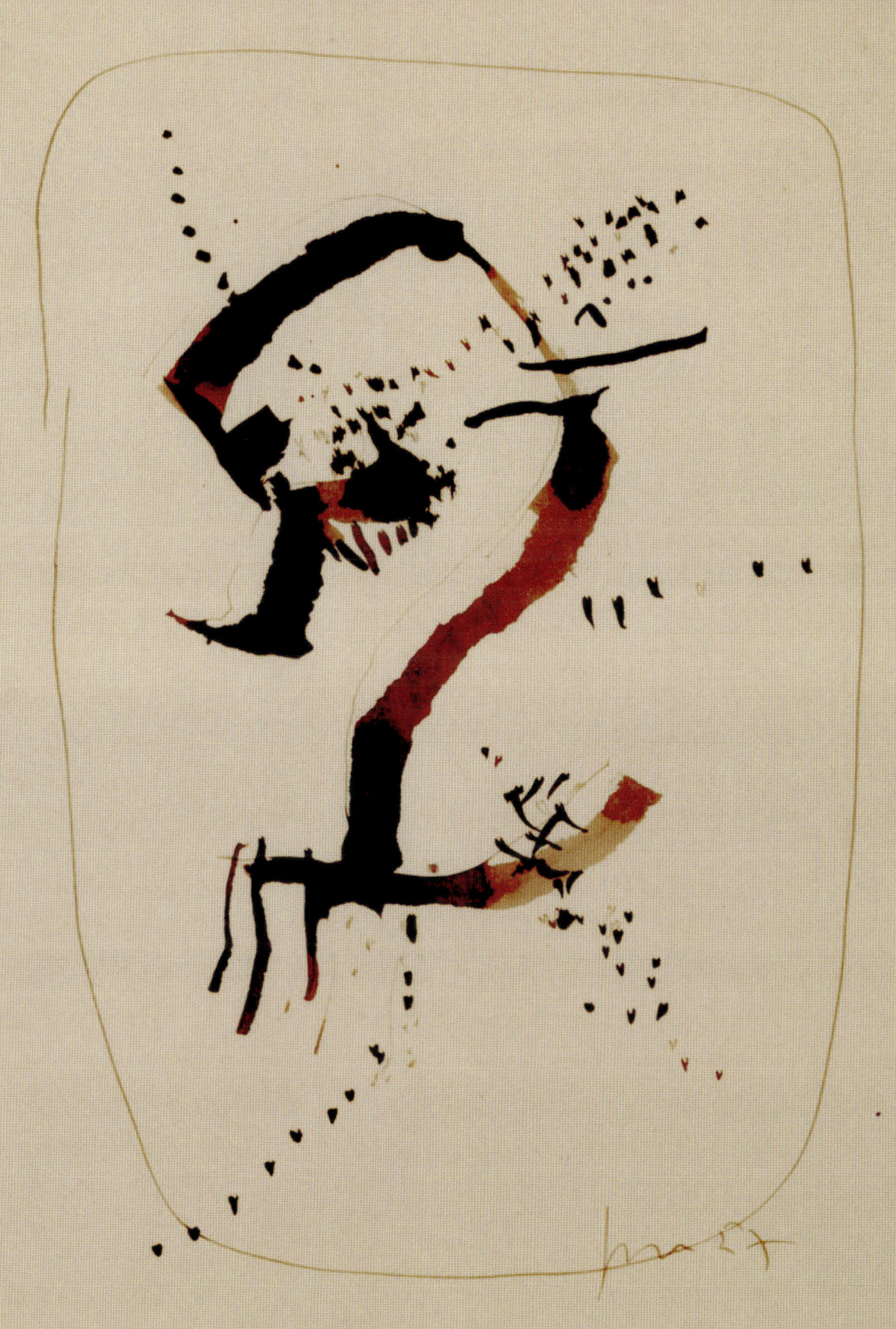

CONCETTO SPAZIALE, ATTESA
[SPATIAL CONCEPT, ATTESA], 1965

Signed, titled, dedicated and inscribed *l. Fontana / 'Concetto Spaziale' / ATTESA / Tu [sic] Al Lerner / l. Fontana / il blu del cielo il / bleu del mare, il san- / gue bleu...* on the reverse
Waterpaint on canvas
54 × 45 cm. (21 1/4 × 17 3/4 in.)

Provenance
Studio Marconi, Milan; Franco Frascarolo Collection, Valenza Po; Private collection, Piedmont; Ben Brown Fine Arts, London ; Private collection, France

Exhibitions
Alessandria, ex Complesso Conventuale di San Francesco, *Lo Sguardo Indiscreto. Arte del XX Secolo dalle Collezioni Alessandrine*, 18 November 2000 - 14 January 2001
Valenza, Villa Scalcabarozzi, *Tesori d'Arte a Valenza. Capolavori dalle Collezioni Private*, 8 December 2013 - 5 January 2014, pp. 122-123

Bibliography
E. Crispolti, *Lucio Fontana, Catalogue Raisonné des Peintures, Sculptures et Environnements Spatiaux*, Edition La Connaissance, Brussels 1974, vol. II, p. 164, no. 65 T 86
E. Crispolti, *Lucio Fontana, Catalogo Generale*, Edizioni Electa, Milan 1986, vol. II, p. 576, no. 65 T 86
E. Crispolti, *Lucio Fontana, Catalogo Ragionato di Sculture, Dipinti, Ambientazioni*, Edizioni Skira, Milan 2006, vol. II, p. 762, no. 65 T 86

SEI STUDI PER TEATRINI (RECTO E VERSO) (SIX SKETCHES FOR TEATRINI [RECTO AND VERSO]), 1964-66

Pen on paper
28 × 22 cm. (11 1/8 × 8 5/8)

Provenance
Private collection, Milan

Exhibitions
London, Ben Brown Fine Arts and Amedeo Porro Arte Moderna e Contemporanea, *From De Chirico to Cattelan: A Survey of 20th Century Italian Art*, 8 October - 30 November 2012, p. 20

Bibliography
L. M. Barbero, *Lucio Fontana. Catalogo Ragionato dei Disegni e delle Carte*, Skira, Milan 2013, vol. III, p. 939, n. 64-65 DSP 310

This work is registered in the *Archivio della Fondazione Lucio Fontana, Milan* under number 1900/205

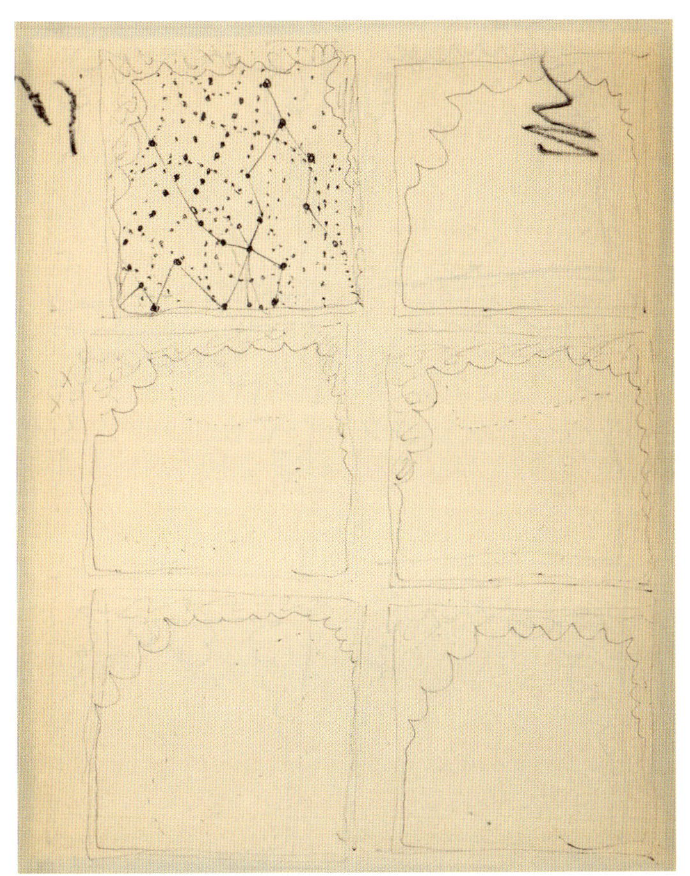

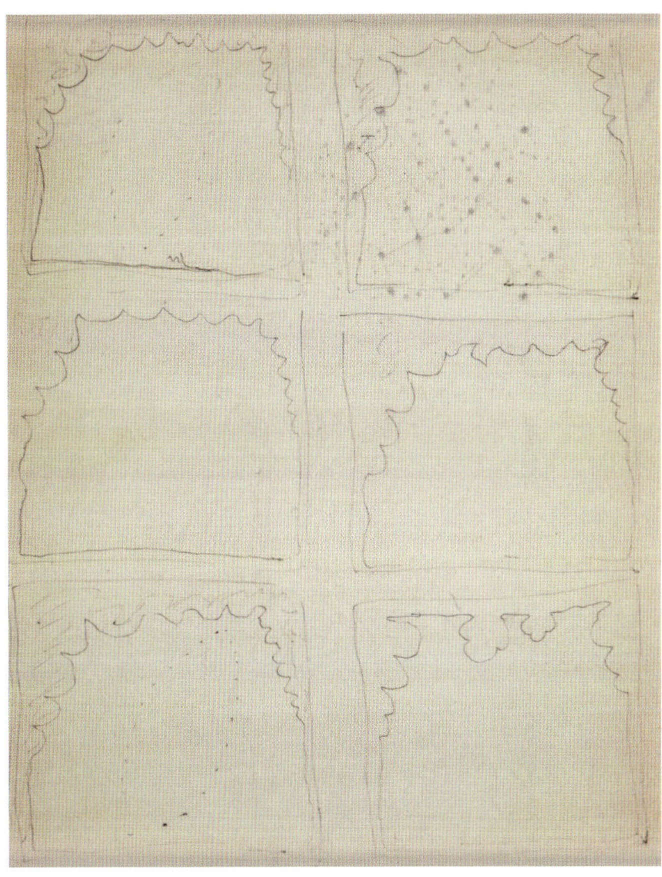

Italian Translations

"...Desidererei presentarmi alla Biennale di Venezia con l'Ambiente spaziale..."

PAOLO CAMPIGLIO

Fin dagli esordi, nella seconda metà degli anni venti, la scelta di Fontana di privilegiare un'arte di ricerca comporta una consapevole opposizione ai contesti provinciali, spesso angusti, e l'apertura a un panorama più vasto, un dialogo a distanza con autori di rilevanza internazionale. In Argentina, nella piccola Rosario è difficile l'aggiornamento sulle ricerche europee, ma l'amico pittore Julio Vanzo, con cui condivide per un periodo lo studio in calle Rioja 2070, lo stimola a guardare, nel 1925, i risultati dell'Esprit Nouveau, le soluzioni di Léger e Le Corbusier, a studiare la "scultopittura" di Archipenko, benché solo visivamente e attraverso uno spoglio forsennato di riviste. Fontana si è formato a Milano e si considera per metà europeo, oltre che argentino, ama il Futurismo, conosce l'opera di Boccioni scultore, che ammirerà per tutta la vita e porrà alle origini dello Spazialismo; ha una passione per Van Gogh e Matisse, di cui forse vede anche delle piccole sculture, ma è sedotto da Archipenko, lo scultore ucraino allora da poco emigrato negli Stati Uniti. Le sue prime opere di ricerca come *Nudo* (1926), in gesso dorato, la *Mujer y el balde* (1926), *Ballerina di Charleston* (1926) esposte al salone del gruppo Nexus a Rosario – una avanguardia di giovani artisti aggiornata sull'arte europea e americana – dichiarano un ragionamento sulla scultura postcubista.

È l'inizio di un percorso di libertà espressiva, scelta a caro prezzo, che lo esporrà alle critiche e alle incomprensioni dei contemporanei, in nome di un concetto più alto dell'arte e di una fede che saranno le uniche ragioni di vita.

L'ulteriore tappa è quella del primo trasferimento in Italia, negli anni renta, luogo di elaborazione e affermazione dei suoi inattesi concetti plastici che il pubblico e la critica non sono in grado di comprendere, se non i pochi estimatori. Tra questi Edoardo Persico e i giovani architetti come Luigi Figini e Gino Pollini, Ernesto Rogers, il gruppo BBPR, che guardano a un orizzonte europeo di Mies Van der Rohe e Le Corbusier. A Milano le ipotesi di Zadkine, Brancusi, la scultura "vitalista" di un artista senza patria come Ernesto De Fiori seducono il giovane Fontana nella ricerca. Già le prime sculture colorate, l'*Uomo nero* (1930), il progetto costruttivista per il monumento a Grandi (1931), le tavolette graffite del 1931, le sculture astratte del 1934 e l'adesione stessa, con Fausto Melotti ad Abstraction-Création nel 1935, indicano come il giovane artista abbia scelto una dimensione internazionale come terreno di confronto, e non solo l'Italia, allora purtroppo radicata in una prospettiva nazionalista.

La produzione in gesso e terracotta colorati, le sculture astratte, rappresentano il primo e aperto dialogo con un contesto europeo, un dialogo sempre vigile e critico che esprime una ipotesi alternativa, mai una dipendenza vera e propria da un linguaggio o dall'altro. Un vitalismo inquieto e libero lo guida nell'oscillazione tra figurazione e astrazione nella convinzione che sia il fatto plastico a parlare come emanazione della propria umanità: è la realtà dell'opera a determinare il fatto artistico e non solo le ragioni teoriche che la sottendono. Ed egli cerca altro, non lo soddisfa l'ambiguità di certo Astrattismo geometrico, del Surrealismo ama il disegno automatico, il graffito, ma non l'iconografia dell'inconscio, spesso abusata, e non accetta la rivoluzione sociale auspicata da Breton: egli intende superare il volume, aggirare le separazioni tra scultura e pittura, ma con un percorso tortuoso, che lo porta a contraddire anche Brancusi. E il colore, che per Fontana rappresenta la luce che annulla il volume, assume un valore determinante in questa liberazione delle forme: il rosso, il rosa, l'azzurro, il violetto e il verde pistacchio, il bianco e il nero, l'oro e l'argento sono i toni con cui in questo decennio l'artista ricopre le superfici delle sue opere plastiche e delle sue strutture astratte. Colori mai visti in natura, del tutto artificiali, riconoscibili forse in certi acquerelli di Kandinskij esposti alla Galleria del Milione nel 1934: toni razionalisti e moderni, con un tocco di sensualità e gusto barocco.

L'esperienza della scultura in ceramica, iniziata nel 1936 ad Albisola e continuata nell'autunno del 1937 alla Manufacture de Sèvres, è intesa come ulteriore, straordinaria liberazione della forma e, insieme, come prima ipotesi di confronto internazionale della scultura policroma, nell'ambito di una morfologia neo-naturalista: Fontana intende promuovere la sua ipotesi di scultura in ceramica colorata in Francia e addirittura pensa di trasferirsi stabilmente a Parigi mentre le sue opere in maiolica esposte nel padiglione della Ceramica (con la Manifattura Mazzotti) all'Exposition Iternationale des Arts et des techniques dans la vie moderne, sono premiate. Durante il suo primo soggiorno parigino dall'estate alla fine di novembre del 1937 Fontana viene in contatto con Tristan Tzara e ha una conversazione con Brancusi sul significato del volume: mentre questi insistono sul superamento del "volume" nell'opera scultorea, Fontana oppone il concetto di "spazio" già avviato da Boccioni[1]. L'aneddoto è ripreso nella conversazione di Fontana con Carla Lonzi nel 1967: "Anche dal 1931-1932, già cercavo la scultura a fili, non il volume... avevo fatto discussioni con Brancusi e Tristan Tzara... Io ho un'ammirazione enorme per Brancusi, ma lui è sempre la forma, e io gli ho detto che eran cose stupende dentro in un'epoca, però che c'era già Boccioni con *Muscoli in movimento* (*Forze uniche nella continuità dello spazio*) che ritenevo una scoperta più importante della sua perché, mentre lui valorizzava la materia in un senso scultoreo e anche spaziale, in Boccioni la materia era secondaria, entrava la luce nella materia, dunque niente più preoccupazioni che ci fosse il marmo"[2]. Ma in seguito alle due mostre parigine alla galleria di Madame Jeanne Bucher e alla Galerie Zack, il giovane artista è costretto a fare le valige e a rientrare a Milano: i tempi non sono ancora maturi per un vero e proprio trasferimento, nonostante le sue opere destino una certa ammirazione. Quando Carola Giedion-Welcker include il suo lavoro nel volume *Moderne Plastik: Elemente der Wirklichkeit, Masse und Auflockerung* (1937), pare suscitare un'attenzione internazionale nei confronti della sua opera, ma è solo un'illusione, poiché i successivi anni argentini (1940-1947), ma soprattutto il secondo conflitto mondiale, cancelleranno tutto il lavoro fatto e imporranno a Fontana la necessità di un nuovo inizio. L'ambiente artistico argentino, infatti, appare ancora poco ricettivo, se non nei giovani artisti che lo seguono dopo il 1945, e tuttavia questa sorta di separazione dal mondo europeo serve all'artista come motivo di rilancio e rielaborazione teorica.

Il ritorno dell'artista a Milano, nell'aprile del 1947, date le premesse elaborate a Buenos Aires nel 1946, rappresenta una duplice sfida: con se stesso e con la propria fede ideale nello svecchiamento delle forme e dei mezzi tradizionali dell'arte, al di là del problema della pittura e di quello della scultura, oltre l'astrazione e la figurazione.

È interessante notare, tuttavia come in questo nuovo percorso la ceramica, lungi dall'essere considerata dall'artista come un'eredità del passato, sia, anzi, un costante motivo di rinnovamento, al pari dei suoi primi *Concetti spaziali* inventati nel 1947. Scriveva nel 1948 Lisa Ponti su "Domus", avendo ben presente le esperienze precedenti dell'artista in collaborazione con gli architetti e recensendo una mostra di ceramiche dell'artista:

> Ora Fontana si fa spaziale: vi spiegheremo questo movimento che è apparso nel 1946 a Buenos Aires e nel maggio '47 a Milano con un declamatorio manifesto scritto da letterati, ed ebbe sedute e discussioni negli studi degli architetti Belgioioso e Rogers, al Naviglio e da Sassu: quello che per noi gli dà affidamento è la presenza di Fontana, della sua buona fede, della sua innegabile natura felice [...] Come le avventure più emozionanti, le visioni e le scoperte di tesori, capitano alle persone semplici, che le raccontano in poche parole, così Fontana s'imbarca a piedi sul mare segreto della "scultura spaziale": deve trovare, egli dice, un modo nuovo di scultura che, come la televisione, approfitti dello spazio, del moto e delle luci, ora che tutti i vecchi modi sono esauriti, per ridare vita all'arte[3].

Tale sfida, attraverso i manifesti dello Spazialismo e l'aggregazione di un gruppo di giovani aderenti alla nuova corrente, è lanciata prima di tutto in un ambito nazionale, e in particolare milanese, tra gli architetti e i pochi estimatori Carlo Cardazzo e Milena Milani, Beniamino Joppolo. Tuttavia l'artista anela, come di consueto, a ragionare in una prospettiva più aperta al dialogo tra le discipline e in una dimensione sovranazionale: lo dimostrano le sue partecipazioni alle Biennali di Venezia negli anni cinquanta, che ben rappresentano la contraddizione di fondo tra la volontà di affermazione come protagonista di una linea moderna, il desiderio di essere conosciuto con le opere più sperimentali e radicalmente "spazialiste" e l'angustia del contesto culturale italiano con cui le proposte inevitabilmente si scontrano, a cui fa da corollario la contemporanea incomprensione della critica internazionale.

Fontana aveva già esposto alla Biennale di Venezia nel lontano 1930, ma era stata una occasione di prima notorietà ancora voluta dal maestro Wildt che era in commissione, a cui era seguito un silenzio durato 18 anni.

Nel primo appuntamento internazionale del Dopoguerra, alla XXIV Biennale di Venezia del 1948, l'artista si presenta con cinque opere: tre in ceramica, il grande *Gallo* (1948) in mosaico poi acquistato dalla Galleria Nazionale di Roma e soprattutto *Scultura spaziale* (1947). Opere in ceramica, mosaico e opere spaziali, a ribadire la contiguità delle ricerche. In questa anti-scultura (a cui fa da corollario il *Concetto spaziale* [1947] sorta di figura umana mutilata, greve, metafora dell'uomo dell'era atomica) l'artista affronta il problema di rappresentare lo spazio mediante una materia che disegna una corona circolare, un anello, lasciando che il vuoto divenga protagonista al centro della composizione: è un ritorno ai primordi, al primo uomo sulla terra, in un'immagine che può ricondurre al principio del mondo come alludere a un futuro nello spazio, alla lenta rarefazione di materiali galattici o a un luminoso fungo atomico. L'opera tuttavia non è notata alla mostra internazionale e non desta alcuna reazione nella critica che frequenta l'esposizione veneziana.

L'indagine nucleare "spaziale", è ripresa nel 1948 e 1949, in alcune gouache in preparazione dell'*Ambiente spaziale* (1949) alla Galleria del Naviglio di Milano, come in un gruppo di ceramiche in cui il vortice diviene metafora di un gorgo materico, di una concentrazione della massa[4]. Se l'*Ambiente spaziale* (1949) per la sua sorprendente novità, suscita la reazione della stampa italiana, pur nella breve durata di solo cinque giorni, e ottiene l'obiettivo previsto di promuovere la prima manifestazione pubblica del Movimento spaziale, l'unica testata a diffusione internazionale che nel maggio dello stesso anno pubblica in copertina una bella riproduzione a colori dell'invenzione fontaniana è "Domus", diretta da Gio Ponti.

Non c'è da stupirsi, quindi, che l'obiettivo dell'artista sia quello di riproporre *l'Ambiente spaziale* alla XXV Biennale di Venezia del 1950 (o di crearne uno nuovo), dove è invitato, per dare un messaggio più incisivo e spettacolare. Fontana, in particolare, scrive a Rodolfo Pallucchini il 19 novembre 1949, da Albisola[5]:

> Egregio Signore / desidererei presentarmi alla Biennale di Venezia con l'"Ambiente Spaziale" perciò la prego abbia la cortesia comunicare ai membri della Commissione d'inviti questa mia richiesta. Se Lei, o la Commissione crede opportuno posso inviarle in forma più [cancellato] dettaglia-

> ta quale siano le mie intenzioni e le ragioni della polemica Spaziale. / In attesa di una di Lei risposta distintamente la saluto / Lucio Fontana / Via Piccinni 1 / Milano / N.B. Albissola Capo / Ristorante Pescetto / Savona.

È del 26 novembre 1949 la risposta di Pallucchini a Fontana, indirizzata al ristorante "Pescetto" di Albisola Capo[6]:

> Egregio Signore, / Se la Sua lettera del 19 corr. mi fosse giunta qualche tempo prima, l'avrei senz'altro comunicata alla Commissione, chiedendoLe magari di mandarmi dell'altro materiale illustrativo sull'ambiente e sulla polemica spaziale da aggiungere a quello che del resto è già in possesso del nostro Archivio Storico d'Arte Contemporanea; ma la Commissione si è riunita il 12 e il 13 e quindi parecchi giorni prima ch'Ella mi scrivesse. / In quelle sedute è stato definito il piano della Mostra e sono state formulate le proposte da sottoporre alla Presidenza per gli inviti. Pur non potendo, per ovvie ragioni, metterla a parte dettagliatamente di quanto è stato deciso nei suoi riguardi, ritengo di poter pensare ch'Ella non sarà scontento di ciò che fra non molto Le verrà comunicato ufficialmente. / Voglia gradire i miei migliori saluti.

Svanita la possibilità di creare un ambiente, l'artista espone alla Biennale del 1950 ancora sculture in ceramica, produzione a cui in questo momento è legata la sua rara visibilità internazionale. Una visibilità che l'artista rende molto più esplicita, invece, in occasione della seconda realizzazione ambientale, dal carattere programmatico, dopo l'*Ambiente spaziale*: il *Concetto spaziale* alla IX Triennale di Milano (1951), la linea continua di luce al neon che si svolge, a notevole altezza, contro il soffitto azzurro della Triennale milanese progettato dagli architetti Baldessari e Grisotti. L'opera è infatti riprodotta allora da riviste internazionali di architettura come la newyorchese "Interiors" e l'artista è tra i relatori del Convegno Internazionale delle Proporzioni (1951) dove presenta il proprio *Manifesto tecnico* a fianco di Le Corbusier, Max Bill, Vantongerloo per sostenere le ragioni della propria arte.

È del 14 settembre 1951, sulla scia del successo del *Concetto spaziale* della IX Triennale, il secondo tentativo da parte di Fontana di dar vita a un *Ambiente spaziale* nell'ambito della XXVI Biennale di Venezia del 1952 come si legge in una nuova lettera inviata a Pallucchini[7]:

> Milano 14 settembre 1951 / Prof. Rodolfo Pallucchini / Segretario Generale Biennale Venezia / Egregio Professore, / mi rivolgo a Lei, perché abbia la cortesia di appoggiare la mia richiesta presso la Commissione d' inviti per la prossima Biennale, e ottenere un piccolo spazio per realizare [sic] l' "Ambiente Spaziale" cosa che non fu possibile nell'ultima Biennale essendo la mia richiesta giunta troppo tardi. / Scritti, polemiche e opere (foto) realizzate dagli spaziali io le terrei a loro disposizione in caso di richiesta./Mi permetto metterla al corrente che in Francia s'è formato di recente un movimento firmato da architetti e artisti chiamato "Groupe Espace", i concetti sono i medesimi enunciati nei manifesti del 1947 e 1948 dal Gruppo italiano. Perciò spero che la mia richiesta ora non rientri in un ordine fantasioso e venga presa in considerazione. / Ringraziandola cordialmente, la saluto / Lucio Fontana / Via Prina 7

La risposta di Pallucchini inviata a Fontana il 17 settembre 1951 in via Prina 7 a Milano appare in un primo momento favorevole[8]:

> Venezia, 17 settembre 1951/ Preg.mo Fontana, ho ricevuto la Sua lettera del 14 e desidero darle assicurazione di aver preso buona nota di quanto Ella mi ha esposto in essa e che io non mancherò di sottoporre alla Commissione, la quale avrà cura di ordinare la mostra / Voglia gradire i miei più cordiali saluti

Ma in seguito alla rinuncia di Alberto Magnelli di far parte della Commissione esecutiva della XXVI Biennale, Pallucchini suggerisce il nome di Fontana come commissario, che accetta di partecipare anche nell'intento di promuovere il gruppo Spazialista. La commissione, presieduta da Roberto Longhi, con la partecipazione di Pallucchini comprendeva Pericle Fazzini e Carlo Alberto Petrucci, membri del Comitato Internazionale di Esperti, tra cui Luigi Montanarini allora rappresentante della Federazione Nazionale Sindacati Autonomi Arti Figurative e Publio Morbiducci, rappresentante della CISL, Paolo Ricci, rappresentante della CGIL, e gli artisti Enrico Paolucci, Enrico Prampolini, Giuseppe Santomaso. Nelle riunioni veneziane tra le prime decisioni messe ai voti in commissione, a cui Fontana e Santomaso sono contrari, è l'esclusione degli artisti commissari dalla mostra: così sfuma immediatamente il progetto di un nuovo *Ambiente spaziale*. Fontana e Fazzini, inoltre, sin dalla prima riunione, propongono una retrospettiva su Balla, fortemente osteggiata dagli altri commissari, criticando, invece, la candidatura di Sironi, Casorati, Rosai: dal verbale, infatti, risulta che l'artista "dice che questi 'anziani' dieci anni fa hanno avuto delle sale alla Biennale e ora sarebbe giusto dare le sale ai giovani". Per quanto riguarda le sale personali ai giovani l'orientamento sostenuto, tra gli altri, da Santomaso è quello del gruppo dell'"astratto-concreto' che verrà presentato da Lionello Venturi, a cui afferiscono Afro, Birolli, Cassinari, Morlotti, tra gli altri, ma Fontana non ritiene Vedova all'altezza di Birolli e Cassinari, sostenendo invece Aligi Sassu e, tra gli scultori, Agenore Fabbri. Nella successiva riunione, in vista di un allargamento della partecipazione ai cosiddetti "giovanissimi" Fontana "pone il problema degli 'spaziali'" e "a richiesta di qualche commissario illustra queste nuove tendenze degli artisti spaziali e nucleari e fa dei nomi che sono per Milano: Dova, Peverelli, Crippa, Dangelo, Baj, Dorazio, Carozzi e Joppolo". In un secondo momento Fontana "si batte a lungo per i milanesi astrattisti, di vecchia data, soprattutto in relazione a i romani"[9], ma la sua proposta non è accettata dalla maggioranza. Gli viene concesso solo di sostituire Lilloni con Spilimbergo. Degli spazialisti esporranno solo Crippa e Dova, mentre Peverelli, invitato per la grafica, rifiuterà.

Alla Biennale successiva, la XXVII edizione (1954), invitato come scultore con una sala personale, Fontana non pensa più all'*Ambiente spaziale* ma per la prima volta immagina una sua esposizione retrospettiva, con un allestimento di pareti verdi e basi nere per le sculture: l'importante è che in questa prima visione storica del proprio lavoro egli insista per porre in relazione la ricerca pre-spaziale delle sue tavolette graffite del 1931 o delle sculture astratte del 1934 con l'ultima produzione spazialista del 1952, in particolare i concetti spaziali forati, a sottolineare la continuità della ricerca tra anni trenta e anni cinquanta. La sala, che alla fine è di 18 opere, è ricordata ancora nel 1957 dal critico Valsecchi come un vero scandalo, non solo perché l'artista contraddice la tradizionale separazione tra scultura e pittura, ma perché i suoi concetti spaziali forati su carta, cartone o tela non rientrano né nell'astrazione geometrica né in un realismo figurativo e risultano incomprensibili ai più, nonostante la presentazione in catalogo di Giampiero Giani. Tanto è vero che, come si ricava dal carteggio con Pallucchini, i quadri spaziali vengono "malmenati villanamente" dal pubblico i "fori strappati e manomessi" per tutta la durata dell'esposizione, con grave risentimento da parte dell'artista. La sala, tuttavia, nonostante le polemiche suscitate, non ha ancora alcun riscontro nella stampa internazionale[10].

L'esperienza storica del 1954 rappresenta in un certo senso la premessa dell'invito più ampio alla XXIX Biennale del 1958, dove Fontana organizza una importante sala personale che, questa volta, trova un inedito interesse non solo da parte della cultura francese, ma anche da parte del mondo anglosassone. Il nuovo circuito che si apre in particolare verso Londra si rivelerà di importanza cruciale per Lucio ed è dovuto essenzialmente all'impegno e all'amicizia di un collezionista, mecenate, manager di primo piano come Carlo Damiano, italo-argentino allora dirigente della Pirelli House di Londra. Questo snodo internazionale inizia in coincidenza cronologica con la Biennale del 1958, che pertanto rappresenta un momento chiave per la diffusione di una certa immagine dell'artista all'estero. Tra il 1954 e il 1957, infatti, Fontana, oltre ad avere 'trasferito' il problema dell'*Ambiente spaziale* in una serie di collaborazioni spettacolari con l'architettura, sia alla Fiera di Milano che alla Triennale e in commissioni private, soprattutto nell'ambito dei soffitti spaziali, ha diversamente variato il proprio immaginario legato alle opere su tela: in primo luogo con le 'pietre', sempre più elaborate, con frammenti di vetri di Murano applicati sulla tela forata, ha introdotto una dimensione ulteriore di materia luminosa o translucida in dialogo con l'allusione atemporale del foro, in direzione infinita; inoltre ha avviato il ciclo più complesso dei "barocchi", rinnovando il proprio rutilante immaginario materico, per poi, contemporaneamente distendersi – con una fertile dialettica tra materia e anti-materia - nel ciclo dei "gessi", con forme armoniche tondeggianti eseguite con pastelli gessosi, ritagli di tela su tela e una abbassata consistenza materica; infine ha elaborato gli "inchiostri" quadri colorati con aniline, ancora più tenui, con nuove forme di tela ritagliate a collage, dove è evidente, invece, una lirica ispirata al "vuoto" e all'antimateria; sono, come è stato dimostrato, tele *nuagistiche*, che rivelano una sensazione di calma che traspare anche nelle coeve sculture a "gambo" (1957-1958), opere fitomorfe che riprendono le medesime forme traducendole in scultura.

In entrambe queste serie si assiste a un ritorno al puro supporto della tela in una prospettiva di più netta distensione del colore, mentre contemporaneamente riaffiora un'immaginazione di "forme" concluse, dal carattere metaforico e non naturalistico. L'immagine della forma da sempre l'accompagna, dalle prime tavolette graffite in gesso dell'inizio degli anni trenta, ed è come se l'artista ricorresse alle sagome arcuate e al colore, qui più che altrove pittorico, quasi per nostalgia di una "tabula rasa" o di un'alternativa impostazione "formale" e quindi "formativa" dell'opera, caratteristica sempre presente nel suo immaginario. Alcune di queste elaborazioni formali, dall'andamento trasversale, assottigliate in gambi, o steli, che paiono alludere ad alghe o vegetali, sono a lungo studiate dall'artista, in numerosi schizzi, e riproposti nella coeva scultura in ferro.

Dal 4 giugno al 31 luglio 1957, precedentemente alla preparazione della sala alla Biennale, Fontana, grazie all'impegno manageriale dell'amico Damiano, fra i *trustee* della Tate Gallery – in contatto già dalla fine del 1957 con Lawrence Alloway allora assistente del direttore dell'Institute of Contemporary Art (I.C.A.) e con Herbert Read, direttore dell'I.C.A. – , espone con Crippa e Dova alla mostra *Between space and earth. Trends in Italian Art* organizzata per iniziativa di Eric Estorick e Damiano alla Galleria Marlborough di Londra con l'esplicita intenzione di diffondere il movimento spaziale a Londra. L'esposizione è presentata da Alloway che per primo scrive delle opere di Fontana approdate in Regno Unito[11].

La sala della Biennale del 1958, allestita da Carlo Scarpa, oggi nota anche grazie a un servizio del fotografo Giancolombo e dalle riprese di un servizio pubblicato su "Elle", riannoda, come nel 1954, ma in modo più esemplare, il problema della "forma" alle esperienze degli anni trenta: Fontana vi espone ancora due tavolette graffite, inedite, due sculture astratte del 1934 rifatte, pochi "barocchi", tra cui il celebre *Gogotha* di Antonio Boschi, e tante opere nuove, soprattutto "gessi" e inchiostri"[12], alcuni di notevoli dimensioni. La sala magicamente sospesa in un'aura metafisica, dove il filo rosso tra le opere, vecchie e nuove, dà l'effetto di un vero e proprio 'ambiente', sconcerta anche la critica più autorevole e impressiona il giovanissimo Enrico Crispolti: in particolare lo stimola a una lettura diacronica dell'artista, al di là dei pregiudizi e del consueto giudizio legato alla 'trovata'. La presentazione in catalogo di Guido Ballo parla di "essenzialità di pure origini", di "evocazione di spazi indefiniti", sicché l'artista, dopo quell'importante primo successo internazionale, vira ancora la sua produzione verso un'essenzialità nuova, sempre più radicale, che passa attraverso l'esperienza delle 'carte', già tagliate e percorse da lacerazioni, e alla fine del 1958, grazie a questo avvio, giunge ai 'tagli'.

In particolare l'affronto delle 'carte' di cui *Concetto spaziale* (1958) rappresenta una soluzione emblematica, sembra riportare l'artista a quella essenzialità delle prime grandi carte forate a nucleo del 1949: in quelle la rarefazione galattica dei fori esprimeva una soluzione drastica di rinuncia al colore che poteva essere valorizzata inizialmente da una retroilluminazione. E infatti i critici allora parlavano di "schermi". Nelle carte su tela del 1958, di poco antecedenti e contemporanee ai 'tagli', l'artista verifica, invece, la pura sequenzialità di un gesto essenziale entro lo spazio crudo dell'opera. E il gesto è la mano che si muove nello spazio, graffia la superficie bianca della carta forzando la superficie fino al taglio. Un semplice ed elementare processo dunque, una nuova sequenza cifrata in cui l'artista si mette in gioco insieme al linguaggio che usa. In questo senso le 'carte' anticipano i 'tagli' monocromi su tela e ne sono il presupposto.

Nel 1958, intanto, la sua lettura in ambito anglosassone, mediata dalla formulazione critica di Alloway, trova una giustificazione e una singolare interpretazione, come è stato recentemente dimostrato da Francesco Tedeschi[13]: le sue opere del 1957-1958 più legate al concetto di 'forma' vengono interpretate da Alloway in una nuova accezione 'figurativa', non in senso narrativo, ma di formulazione inconscia di nuovi apparati formali che hanno un riscontro nell'immaginario di massa; in ciò distinguendosi rispetto alla lettura contemporanea dell'informale attuata da Greenberg e allora nota. Nel testo di presentazione della mostra *Paintings from Damiano Collection*, esposizione che il manager organizza nel frattempo all'ICA di Londra (7 gennaio - 7 febbraio 1959), dopo aver acquistato dall'artista alcuni 'gessi' e almeno un 'taglio', Alloway interpreta i "buchi" che vede nei 'gessi' non come astruse lacerazioni, ma come segni significanti: "I buchi nei quadri sono di solito segni di rovina, ma i modelli di buchi in Fontana sono formalmente significativi, come un codice, in connessione casuale, ma non ignota, con le schede e i nastri perforati dell'iconografia cibernetica popolare. La struttura dei suoi dipinti è decisamente semplice"[14].

Ma il ruolo di Damiano, che è sempre in contatto con Fontana sia a livello collezionistico (acquisterà dall'artista fino al 1968 circa un'ottantina di opere) sia come amico e grande estimatore della sua opera, va ben oltre il semplice appoggio o l'aiuto nelle traduzioni dei testi critici dall'inglese: dopo il successo della Biennale di Venezia, assistendo alla maturazione ulteriore dell'artista soprattutto in rapporto ai nuovissimi 'tagli', Damiano procura a Fontana il contratto con Mc Robert & Tunnard per un'esclusiva mondiale: si fa personalmente mediatore nella stesura del contratto e nella conduzione dei rapporti commerciali nel mondo anglosassone. La mostra personale di Fontana da Mc Robert & Tunnard organizzata dal 12 ottobre al 5 novembre 1960 e presentata da Alloway è incentrata sui 'tagli', per la prima volta a Londra.

A questa esposizione ne seguiranno altre dirette dall'ingegno di Damiano e alla sua ferma volontà di promuovere Fontana in senso internazionale, tra cui la nota *Ten paintings from Venice* presso Martha Jackson a New York, l'approdo newyorchese di Fontana del 1961, la mostra personale a Leverkusen, a cura di Udo Kultermann realizzata con l'intera collezione Damiano e nata dai contatti del manager con il museo tedesco.

L'iniziale diffusione internazionale dell'artista tra la fine degli anni cinquanta e i primi anni sessanta ha quindi una testa di ponte inglese, oltre all'importante asse tedesco alimentato dai rapporti di Fontana con i giovani del gruppo Zero (Heinz Mack e Otto Piene) e in alternativa al versante francese, a cui tendeva, invece, il gallerista Carlo Cardazzo a partire dal 1959. Non è da trascurare, infatti, il rapporto tra Cardazzo e la galleria Stadler nella presentazione del nuovo ciclo dei 'tagli', offerti in febbraio 1959 al pubblico milanese al Naviglio e poi, in marzo, presso il gallerista parigino con l'avallo dell'autorevole interpretazione critica di Michel Tapié. Si trattò, infatti, di una prima apparizione forse mal orchestrata (l'artista si trovò, a sua insaputa, a dividere la galleria con un artista sudafricano Christo Coetzee) di cui Fontana ebbe a lamentarsi e che convalidava, con l'appoggio di Tapié, una interpretazione ancora informale dell'artista: il 'taglio' come lacerazione e ferita[15]. Il testo di presentazione della successiva mostra dei 'tagli' nel 1960 a Londra, a cura di Alloway, affermava, invece, che: "Fontana is the opposite of hermetic: he is mercurial and outgoing but he is guarded from disappearing into the gulf of sociability which threatens modern Italian artist by a protective core of indifference"[16].

La prima mostra di Fontana *Ten paintings of Venice* a New York da Martha Jackson nell'autunno del 1961 è l'espressione delle sinergie tra Parigi e Londra e Venezia: Tapié dal punto di vista critico concepisce lo studio monografico *Devenir de Fontana*, stampato per le edizioni Fratelli Pozzo di Torino e presentato nelle sale della galleria; il tramite di Damiano e la collaborazione con i galleristi Mc Robert e Tunnard sono i motori primi di quell'approdo newyorchese, così fecondo per la fortuna dell'artista e per il suo lavoro successivo; Venezia, in questa triangolazione, è il luogo, infine, dell'ispirazione di quel ciclo delle 'Venezie' presentato in America e realizzato appositamente da Fontana per la mostra *Arte e contemplazione* organizzata nell'estate del 1961 da Marinotti a Palazzo Grassi.

Occorre infine notare come fin dal 1959 Charles Damiano e la moglie Maria Cambiaghi hanno donato alla Tate Gallery un *Concetto spaziale* di Fontana acquistato alla Biennale di Venezia del 1958, opera che ancora oggi è una parte fondamentale della collezione museale inglese, con l'intento di sollecitare il museo a orientarsi verso l'arte contemporanea italiana. Ma i tempi, forse, non erano ancora maturi e bisognerà attendere ancora alcuni decenni per riscontrare l'attenzione museale all'opera di fontana nel contesto inglese.

[1] Michel Tapié, *Dévenir de Fontana*, Edizioni Fratelli Pozzo, Torino 1961. L'aneddoto riportato da Tapié intende porre in evidenza la prematura riflessione dell'artista intorno allo spazio della scultura, piuttosto che al superamento del volume.
[2] C. Lonzi, *Autoritratto*, Bari 1969, p. 168.
[3] L. Ponti, *Prima astratto, poi barocco, ora spaziale*, in "Domus", n. 229, Volume quarto, 1948, p. 36.
[4] Si tratta del nucleo di sculture siglate nel Catalogo Generale con la sigla 49 SC 3 – 49 SC 7.
[5] ASAC, Serie Arti Visive, scat. 23, fasc. F 1949-50, pubblicata in P. Campiglio (a cura di), *Lucio Fontana.Lettere 1919-1968*, Edizioni Skira, Milano 1999, p. 150.
[6] ASAC, Serie Arti Visive, scat. 23, fasc. F 1949-50.
[7] ASAC, Serie Arti Visive, scat. 38, fasc.Commissione esecutiva, Fontana Lucio, pubblicata in P. Campiglio (a cura di), *Lucio Fontana.Lettere 1919-1968*, cit. p. 150.
[8] ASAC, Serie Arti Visive, scat. 38, fasc.Commissione esecutiva, Fontana Lucio
[9] ASAC, Venezia, verbali stenografici, Scarpa 7, XXVI Biennale di Venezia. Prima seduta della commissione esecutiva 3712/1951 e seconda seduta della commissione secutiva 19-20/12/1951.
[10] La vicenda è analizzata da G. Zanchetti, *Lucio Fontana, Concetto spaziale, 1957*, in *Esercizi di Lettura*, Edizioni Skira, Milano 2002, pp. 181-203.
[11] La mostra comprendeva anche opere di Ajmone, Bacci, Birolli, Brunori, Capogrossi, Chighine, Corpora, Morandi, Moreni, Morlotti, Negri.
[12] G. Zanchetti, *Lucio Fontana, Concetto spaziale, 1957*, cit. pp. 191-198.
[13] F. Tedeschi, *L'opera di Fontana tra gli anni Cinquanta e Sessanta e la sua ricezione nell'ambiente inglese*, in *Lucio Fontana Beyond Space*, Imago art Gallery, 19 ottobre -16 dicembre 2008, pp. 16-27.
[14] L. Alloway, *Paintings from Damiano Collection, ICA, London, catalogo della mostra,* 7 gennaio - 7 febbraio 1959.
[15] Scriveva Pierre Restany in quell'occasione che "La cosa più triste è che sia stato imposto a Fontana un tale accostamento per la sua prima mostra importante a Parigi. Qui la personalità di Fontana è poco conosciuta. [ ] L'ampiezza del personaggio, il suo passato, l'apertura delle sue ricerche, tutto questo meritava di meglio o per lo meno un'altra presentazione. Le opere esposte erano tutte recenti: tele generalmente monocrome, bucate da lacerazioni longitudinali. Sta tutto lì, nell'affermazione del gesto. Ma in un contesto così aggressivamente barocco come quello di Coetzee questo gesto perdeva tutta la sua ampiezza". P. *Restany, Fontana, Coetzee, Tàpies*, "Cimaise", 5 giugno, luglio, agosto 1959, p. 46, riportato in S. Bignami J. Galimberti, *Lucio Fontana e L'artventure parigina*, Scalpendi editore, 2014, p. 16.
[16] L. Alloway, *Lucio Fontana*, London, Mc Robert & Tunnard, 12 ottobre - 5 novembre 1960.

Antologia critica

Una breve antologia critica raduna i testi difficilmente reperibili di presentazione delle prime mostre di Lucio Fontana a Londra e a New York dal 1957 al 1962, a cura di Lawrence Alloway e Pierre Rouve. I testi sono contemporanei alla diffusione dei *Concetti spaziali* nel contesto artistico britannico e americano. L'antologia riporta il giudizio espresso da Alloway sulle opere di Fontana, alcune di collezione Damiano, presenti nella mostra collettiva *Between space and earth. Trends in Italian Art*, organizzata per iniziativa di Eric Estorick e Carlo Damiano alla Galleria Marlborough di Londra, 4 giugno - 31 luglio 1957; è riprodotta inoltre la parte relativa a Fontana, sempre a cura di Alloway in *Painting from the Damiano Collection Fontana, Dova, Crippa, Clemente*, catalogo della mostra ICA, Londra, 7 gennaio - 7 febbraio 1959; Il commento del critico inglese alla prima traduzione del *Manifesto Tecnico dello Spazialismo* (1951), con data errata al 1947, pubblicato su "ARK" alla fine del 1959 o ai primi del 1960; la presentazione, sempre a cura di Alloway, della prima esposizione dei 'tagli' di Fontana a Londra nella mostra organizzata da Mc Roberts & Tunnard, 12 ottobre - 5 novembre 1960; il saggio di Pierre Rouve in *Fontana paintings 1962*, Mc Robert & Tunnard, novembre-dicembre 1962.

P.C.

Opere

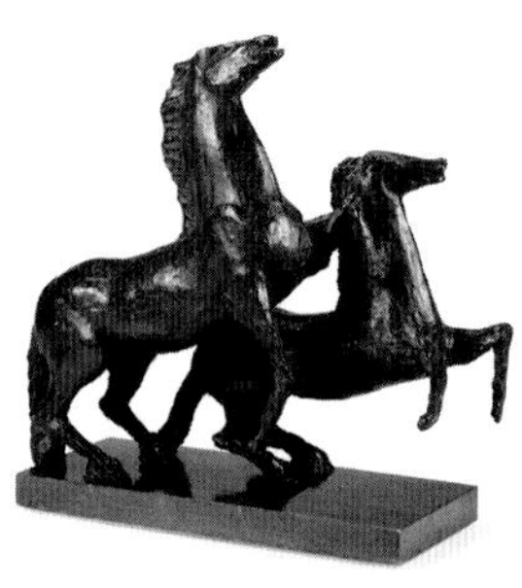

I CAVALLI CHE SEGUONO LA VITTORIA, 1936

Bronzo, esemplare unico
52 × 60 × 25 cm

Provenienza
Milano, collezione privata

Esposizioni
1996 Milano, Museo della Permanente, *Lucio Fontana e Milano,* 11 ottobre - 17 novembre, pp. 54 - 152, n. 8 (erroneamente indicato come gesso patinato);
1999 Milano, Triennale di Milano, *Centenario di Lucio Fontana. Cinque mostre a Milano. Lucio Fontana, la Triennale, la luce,* 23 aprile - 30 giugno, pp. 170-354, n. II, 14.
2003 Leeds - Rovereto, Henry Moore Institute, 31 maggio - 31 agosto; MART, 28 ottobre -14 dicembre, Dead Language *Sculpture. Sculpture from fascist Italy; Scultura Lingua Morta: Scultura nell'Italia fascista,* Henry Moore Institute-Mart, p. 98, n. 5.

Bibliografia
P. Campiglio, *Lucio Fontana. La scuola architettonica degli anni Trenta,* Ilisso, Nuoro 1995, pp. 83-84, n. 46;
E. Crispolti, *Fontana,* Edizioni Charta, Milano 1999, pp. 114, 115, n. 44.
E. Crispolti, *Lucio Fontana. Catalogo ragionato di sculture, dipinti, ambientazioni,* Edizioni Skira, Milano 2006, vol. II, p. 935, n. 36 A 5.

Tra il 1935 e il 1936 il gruppo di architetti e artisti guidato da Edoardo Persico, con Giancarlo Palanti, Marcello Nizzoli e Lucio Fontana vince il concorso per la decorazione del Salone d'Onore per la VI Triennale di Milano inaugurata nel maggio 1936. Il salone era il punto di maggiore concentrazione simbolica dell'esposizione ufficiale ed era stato concepito da Persico in tono aulico nell'adozione del ritmo continuo di alte quinte che sintetizzavano, in senso astratto, l'idea del colonnato antico. L'ambiente completamente bianco e isolato dal resto dell'architettura era illuminato artificialmente ed emanava un chiarore spettrale. Fontana ha immaginato, entro lo spazio razionale progettato da Persico, un notevole gruppo plastico in gesso su un alto basamento costituito da una figura allegorica avanzante in primo piano, che rappresenta l'Italia fascista, seguita da un simbolo antico dell'energia e del dinamismo: due cavalli rampanti. Ma la risoluzione della campagna di occupazione dell'Etiopia, nei mesi di preparazione dell'esposizione, imponeva per ordine delle autorità di cambiare il titolo dell'opera in *Vittoria,* costringendo ad apporre una frase di Mussolini alla base del gruppo. Una serie di fotomontaggi di Nizzoli con ritratti di imperatori romani, all'ingresso, dava all'ambiente l'ufficialità richiesta dalla committenza, con una tecnica moderna.
Il bozzetto per i cavalli, in bronzo patinato, che fu presentato da Fontana come prova per la commissione, indica l'originario intento dell'artista di adottare un colore astratto (una acromia bianca o nera) su una base figurativa dalla forte sintesi dinamica, a sottolineare l'identità problematica tra astrazione e figurazione. Il tema antico del cavallo rampante come simbolo dell'energia e del dinamismo, rivalutato in ambito futurista, viene personalmente interpretato da Fontana come emblema di una massa in movimento articolata nello spazio, fin dalle prime sculture degli anni trenta; in futuro il cavallo rampante, il cosiddetto "el caballo loco", resta un soggetto caro all'artista, in ceramica, simbolo di energia irrazionale, emblema della pura manifestazione della forza in movimento, quasi una memoria del passato da 'gaucho' trascorso nella pampa argentina.

Una nota di Enrico Crispolti dal *Lucio Fontana. Catalogo ragionato di sculture, dipinti, ambientazioni,* Edizioni Skira 2006, p. 53
[...] In questi anni, dopo le collaborazioni dei primi Trenta, anche i suoi interessi di scultore in rapporto con l'architettura si arricchiscono di nuove e più consistenti esperienze.
[...] Nella prima metà del 1936 realizza il grande gruppo plastico per il Salone della Vittoria nella VI Triennale di Milano (la Vittoria seguita da Cavalli rampanti eseguiti in gesso). Notevolissimo episodio di caratterizzazione ambientale nella corrente architettonica razionalistica italiana "semplice limite di spazio in cui alzare un'opera del tutto indipendente e originale" scriveva Edoardo Persico nella relazione concorsuale. [...] Fontana dunque concorreva con i propri specifici mezzi meccanici a quell'evento di monumentalità pulita e razionale, schiettamente antiretorica e perciò opposta al trionfalismo dominante nell'architettura ufficiale del regime fascista, "post-novecentesca" ma ormai anche spesso di compromesso razionalista.

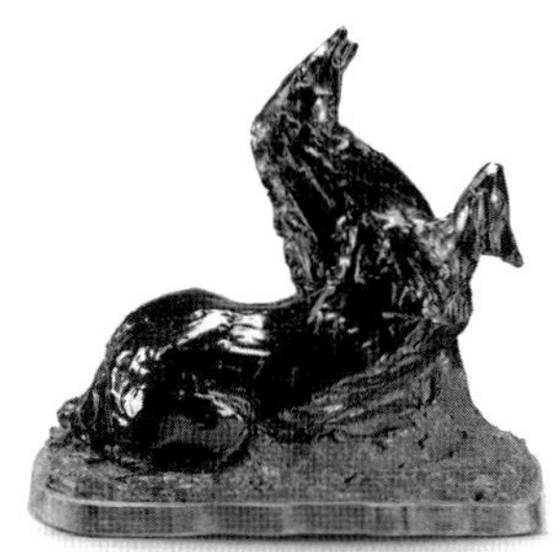

CAVALLO, 1936

Ceramica colorata, invetriata, nera con riflessi verdi, base in legno
52 × 51 × 33 cm

Provenienza
Milano, collezione privata

Esposizioni
1996 Milano, Museo della Permanente, *Lucio Fontana e Milano*, 11 ottobre - 17 novembre, pp. 94-152, n. 9.

Bibliografia
E. Crispolti, *Lucio Fontana. Catalogo ragionato di sculture, dipinti, ambientazioni*, Edizioni Skira, Milano 2006, vol. I, p. 166, n. 36 SC 10.

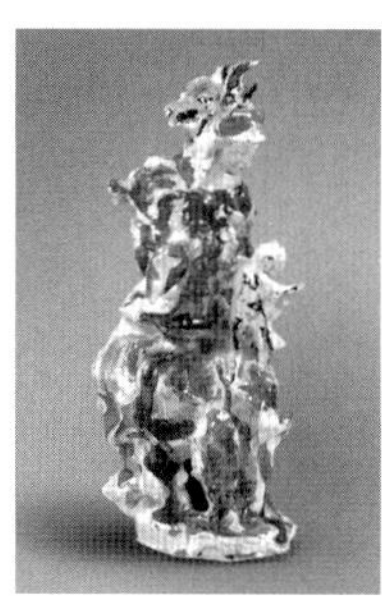

MADONNA CON BAMBINO, 1950-1955

Ceramica colorata, riflessata, bianca e blu con riflessi dorati
40 × 17 × 20 cm
Iniziali incise lungo la base: *l. f.*

Provenienza
Legnano (Mi), collezione privata

Opera registrata presso l'Archivio della Fondazione Lucio Fontana, Milano con il numero 250/2.

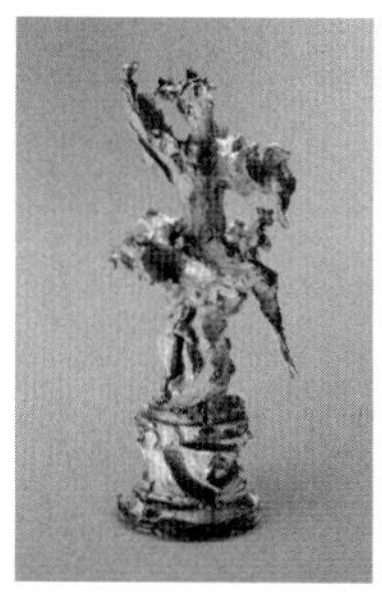

BALLERINA, 1952

Ceramica dipinta, bianco, rosa e nero
91 × 41 × 32,5 cm
Firma e data incise nella parte superiore della base: *l. fontana / 52*
Iniziali *L.F.* incise nella parte inferiore della base

Provenienza
Trivero (Vercelli), collezione privata

Esposizioni
1955 Madrid, Palacio del Reitiro, *Exposicion de Arte Italiano Contemporaneo*, Biennal Hispano-Americana de Arte, maggio - giugno, p. 50, n. 7

Bibliografia
E. Crispolti, *Lucio Fontana. Catalogo Generale*, Edizioni Electa, Milano 1986, vol. I, p 158 n. 52 SC 18;
E. Crispolti, *Lucio Fontana. Catalogo Ragionato di sculture, dipinti, ambientazioni*, Edizioni Skira, Milano 2006, vol. I, p. 298, n. 52 SC 18.

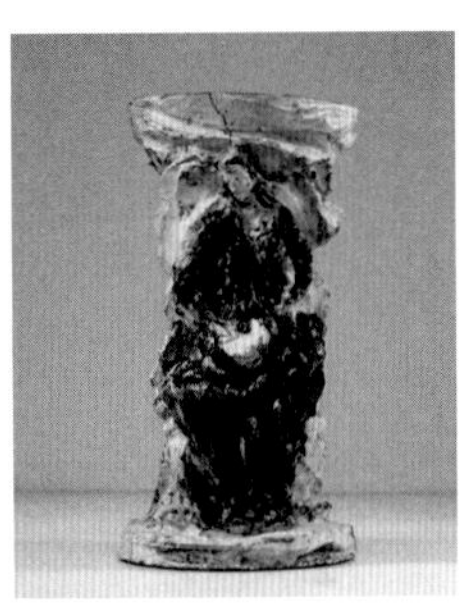

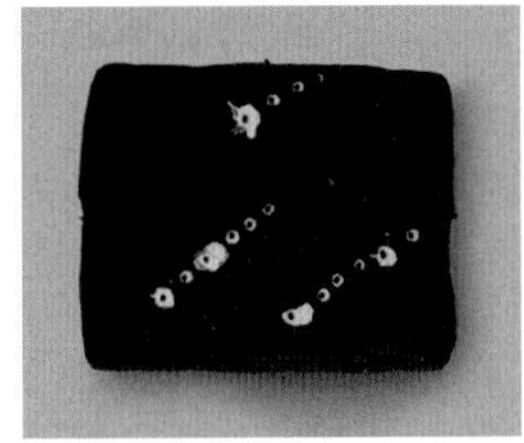

BASE PER TAVOLO CON DECORAZIONI FLOREALI E FIGURA FEMMINILE, 1952

Terracotta smaltata colorata bianco, giallo e nero
64 × 36 × 36 cm
Firma e data incise lungo la base: *l. fontana '52*

Provenienza
Milano, collezione privata

Opera registrata presso l'Archivio della Fondazione Lucio Fontana, Milano con il numero 3724/1.

CONCETTO SPAZIALE, 1954

Buchi e graffito su terracotta colorata a freddo, bianco e nero
25 × 31 cm
Firma e data incise in basso a destra: *l. Fontana 54*

Provenienza
Milano, collezione privata

Esposizioni
2007 Milano, Amedeo Porro arte moderna e contemporanea, *Lucio Fontana, Sedici Sculture 1937-1967*, 12 dicembre - 28 febbraio, fig. 7, pp. 90-91; Londra, Ben Brown Fine Arts, aprile-maggio;
2012 Londra, Ben Brown Fine Arts e Amedeo Porro Arte moderna contemporanea, *From De Chirico to Cattelan. A Survey of 20th Century Italian Art*, 8 ottobre - 30 novembre, p. 18.

Bibliografia
E. Crispolti, *Lucio Fontana, Catalogo ragionato di sculture, dipinti, ambientazioni*, Edizioni Skira, Milano 2006, vol. I, n. 54 SC 10, p. 307.

La produzione di "sculture spaziali" in forma di tavolette in terracotta, segnate da gocce di colore a freddo e forate, risale ai primi anni cinquanta, ma si intensifica nel 1954. È probabile che la serie realizzata in quell'anno in una trentina di pezzi sia da porre in relazione al desiderio di confrontarsi con la ceramica di Jorn, Appel, Corneil radunati in quell'estate all'*Incontro Internazionale dei Ceramisti* di Albisola: all'espressionismo dei Cobra Fontana oppone una ceramica "silenziosa", parallela ai *Concetti spaziali* forati su tela. Certamente l'occasione della sala retrospettiva alla XXVII Biennale di Venezia (1954), dove Fontana espone le sue prime tavolette graffite del 1931 insieme alle tele ultime può aver contribuito a una ripresa della tavoletta graffita.
Se nella serie delle "pietre" i frammenti di vetro colorati e incollati alla tela costituiscono l'elemento luminoso in dialogo con le traiettorie delle perforazioni, nelle tavolette, dalle sequenze rettilinee di fori, in senso diagonale, la luce è resa attraverso la semplice macchia di colore, con una evidente essenzialità. In questo esempio in terracotta colorata d'un nero opaco, con bianche gocce di smalto, le sequenze parallele di perforazioni (di differente diametro) tracciate nello spazio monocromo in diagonale, sono evidenziate solo in parte dalle sgocciolature sovrapposte, creando l'illusione spaziale di un dialogo tra elementi muti ed elementi squillanti.
Qui si ha una essenziale bicromia bianco/nero, ma altre ipotesi della medesima serie prevedono sgocciolature di differenti tonalità, solo circoscritte ai fori, in grado di contrastare il vuoto espresso dalle perforazioni. Con tale espediente, basato sulla semplicità e sul gioco, Fontana esprime una calma e distesa immaginazione spaziale, quasi di un cielo stellato o di una apparizione cosmica, che troverà una più compiuta espressione nel successivo ciclo dei "gessi" e degli "inchiostri".

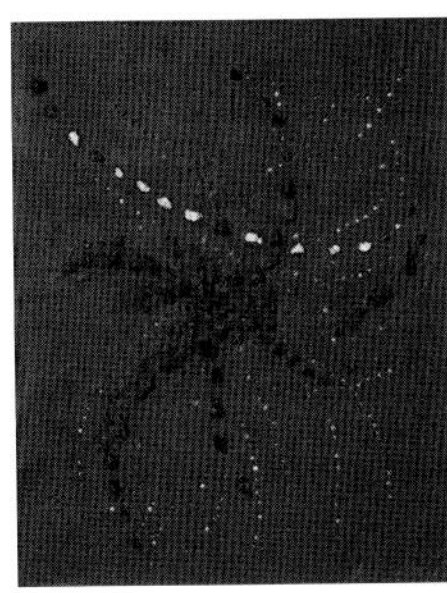

CONCETTO SPAZIALE, 1955

Olio, buchi, pietre e idropittura su tela, nero con accenni rossi, pietre bianche e nere
50 × 40 cm
Firma e data incise in basso a destra:
l. fontana 55.

Provenienza
Roma, collezione privata

Opera registrata presso l'Archivio della Fondazione Lucio Fontana, Milano con il numero 2838/1.

Mentre nel 1955 l'artista lavora intensamente nella ceramica per preparare tre mostre, di cui una celebre alla Galleria San Fedele di Milano dedicata esclusivamente all'opera sacra, nello studio di Corso Monforte 23 sviluppa il ciclo delle 'pietre' in una serie notevole di *Concetti spaziali* caratterizzati dall'uso di frammenti di vetri colorati incollati sulla tela e verniciati. Cinque *Concetti spaziali* di questa serie, esposti alla Quadriennale di Roma del 1955, rappresentano la pubblicazione più esplicita del ciclo e la sua prima diffusione in ambito non specialistico.
Il *Concetto spaziale* (1955) presenta un motivo formale al centro, una massa di materia realizzata con un gruppo di vetri incollati alla tela, tutti verniciati del medesimo tono grigio dello sfondo e resi opachi da un'abbondanza di materia pittorica.
La forma ad andamento stellare e curvilineo, appare in espansione in cinque direzioni con alcune scie di materiali vetrosi. Il motivo galattico è attraversato però da due sequenze di elementi vetrosi lucidi, una scia bianca di luce che segna la tela orizzontalmente e una perpendicolare di vetri più scuri. A questa forma fa da contrappunto una serie di perforazioni di dimensioni diverse e di sezione stellare o circolare con andamento curvilineo e festoso che seguono le traiettorie dinamiche suggerite dall'elemento centrale. Lo spazio grigio della tela è un'allusione alla volta celeste in cui si manifesta l'apparizione cosmica, ma è anche lo spazio della compenetrazione tra materia e anti-materia, tra fisicità cupa di un materiale grezzo e luminosità di alcune traiettorie, tra una superficie ancora tangibile e andamenti armonici di punti che alludono allo spazio infinito.
Il particolare *Informel* di Fontana è caratterizzato dalla costruzione di una forma, pure immaginata, ma ben riconoscibile, evidenziata dall'andamento dei fori. Il romanticismo creato dalla distribuzione del disegno sulla superficie del quadro, la drammatizzazione espressionista del gesto, lasciano il posto a una pacata orditura che è pura evocazione spaziale.

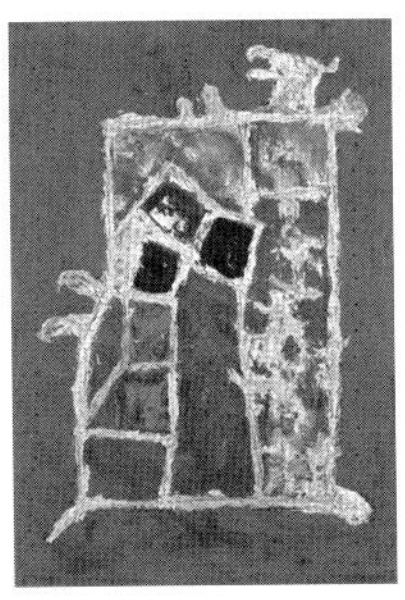

CONCETTO SPAZIALE, 1956

Olio, tecnica mista, buchi e lustrini su tela, forme bianche, verdi e rosse su fondo rosso
134,5 × 100 cm
Firma e data in basso a destra: *l. Fontana 56*
Scritta, titolo, firma e data al retro: *N. 90 /"Concetto spaziale"/ l. fontana / 56*.

Provenienza
New York, Marisa del Re Gallery; Milano, collezione privata; Milano, Galleria Blu; Milano, collezione privata; Milano, Studio Casoli; Milano, collezione privata; Milano, collezione privata; Londra, Fabian Carlsson Gallery.

Esposizioni
1989 Londra, Fabian Carlsson Gallery;
1993 Venezia, *La Biennale di Venezia. LXV Esposizione Internazionale d'Arte*, 11 giugno - 15 ottobre, Marsilio Editore, Venezia, I volume, p. 390.

Bibliografia
Giampaolo, *Fontana*, in "Rossana", a. III, n. 2, Milano 1960, febbraio, pp. 116-117;
E. Crispolti, *Lucio Fontana Catalogue Raisonné des peintures, sculptures et environnements spatiaux*, Edition La Connaissance, Bruxelles 1974, vol. II, pp. 50-51, n. 56 BA 31;
E. Crispolti, *Lucio Fontana. Catalogo Generale*, Edizioni Electa, Milano 1986, vol. I, p. 174, n. 56 BA 31;
E. Crispolti, *Lucio Fontana Catalogo Ragionato di sculture, dipinti, ambientazioni*, Edizioni Skira, Milano 2006, vol. I, p. 327, n. 56 BA 31, riprodotto a colori, vol. I, Tav. CXLIX.

Alcuni *Concetti spaziali* 'barocchi' del 1956 presentano entro lo spazio dipinto non solo una forma inventata, ma un'immagine ben riconoscibile a rilievo, un grande volto o un elemento figurativo stilizzato.
In *Concetto spaziale* del 1956, invece, un perimetro astratto bianco dalla geometria irregolare e dai contorni imprecisi segnati a spatola, che ricorda una planimetria architettonica, include una serie di partizioni e spazi geometrizzanti, lontana memoria

delle linee di Klee. Si tratta di una struttura galleggiante nello spazio rosso da cui si dipartono, lungo il perimetro, degli elementi di forma organica, sorta di peduncoli, agli angoli e nella porzione superiore del dipinto. Qui in particolare, in alto a destra, l'artista sembra alludere alla testa di un animale che lancia un grido, fortemente stilizzata. È una rappresentazione scenica, di carattere surreale e fantastico che si svolge all'interno della più ampia campitura del rosso. Entro la struttura bianca, tra le singole partizioni, la superficie spessa delle paste polimateriche come sabbia, gesso, colla e lustrini, chiarisce il riferimento al Barocco che lo stesso Crispolti, memore della serie di dipinti, ha individuato fin dal 1959 come una costante dell'opera del maestro. L'andamento dei fori, per traiettorie rettilinee e oblique, sembra quasi subordinato alla forma centrale, come un corollario che identifica, tuttavia, un piano spaziale ulteriore nella tonalità dei differenti rossi che ambientano questa apparizione in una spazialità senza confini. In *Concetto spaziale* del 1956 è più evidente il contrasto tra la memoria di una forma, la nozione di un'immagine e l'impossibilità di ricondurre la scena a una scala umana, di immediata comprensione, poiché l'artista lascia agli accostamenti cromatici e alla seduzione delle paste di colore il compito di alludere a una visione fantastica, immaginaria, di pura seduzione. Fontana nel porre in scena un evento, mette in discussione anche il nostro rapporto con la scena, nella convinzione che nello spazio del cosmo gli eventi si svolgano secondo categorie non riducibili a semplici formule matematiche.

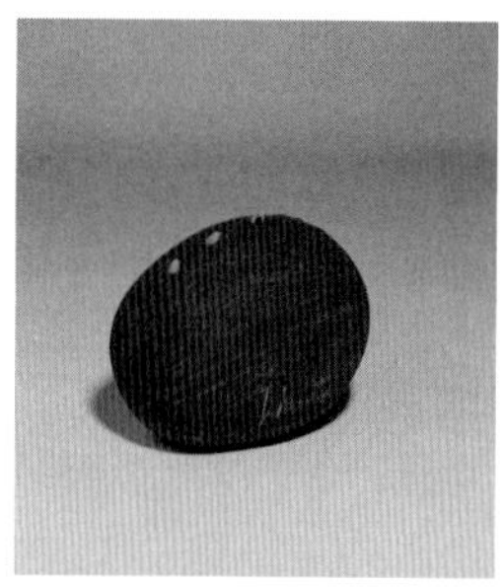

CONCETTO SPAZIALE, 1955-1960

Terracotta con buchi, colorata a freddo, nera
20 × 25,5 × 18,6 cm
Firma incisa sul fianco: *l. fontana*

Provenienza
Parigi, Galerie di Meo

Opera registrata presso l'Archivio della Fondazione Lucio Fontana, Milano con il numero 2368/1.

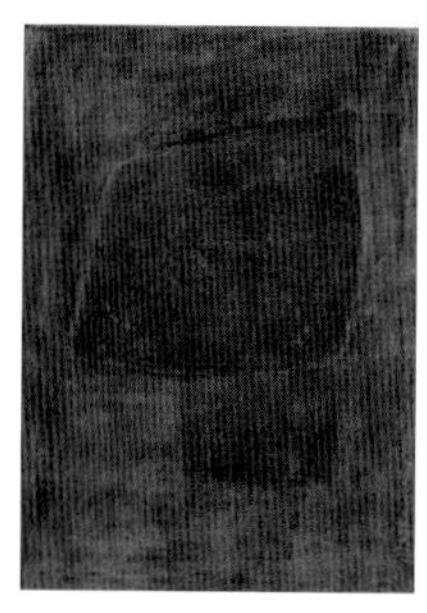

CONCETTO SPAZIALE, 1957

Pastelli e collage su tela forma blu scuro su fondo grigio verde.
100 × 70 cm
Firma e data al retro: *l. fontana / 57*

Provenienza
Milano, Galleria Blu; Milano, collezione privata; Colonia, collezione privata.

Esposizioni
1964 Milano, Galleria Blu, *Fontana*, 5 ottobre - 5 novembre, n. 28;
1972 Milano, Palazzo Reale, *Lucio Fontana*, 19 aprile - 21 giugno, p. 163, fig. 118;
2005 Milano, Palazzo Reale, *Anni Cinquanta. La nascita della creatività italiana*, 4 marzo - 3 luglio, p. 433.

Bibliografia
E. Crispolti, *Lucio Fontana Catalogue Raisonné des peintures, sculptures et environnements spatiaux*, Edition La Connaissance, Bruxelles 1974, vol. II, pp. 56-57, n. 57 G 20;
E. Crispolti, *Lucio Fontana. Catalogo Generale*, Edizioni Electa, Milano 1986, vol. I, p. 196;
R. Pasini, *L'Informale. Stati Uniti – Europa – Italia*, CLUEB, Bologna 1995, fig. 103;
E. Crispolti, *Lucio Fontana. Catalogo Ragionato di sculture, dipinti, ambientazioni*, Edizioni Skira, Milano 2006, vol. I, p. 351, n. 57 G 20.

Nella serie del 'gessi', creata a partire dal 1954, Fontana utilizza i pastelli gessosi per esprimere una nuova distensione della superficie-colore e un particolare effetto intonaco o 'muro'. Ancora nel 1957 alla consistenza materica di tipo barocco egli alterna una rivalutazione della semplice superficie,

di natura tonale in cui prevale la presenza di forme a nucleo o lievitanti. L'artista denominava ironicamente 'panettoni' i quadri con forme arcuate, e 'muri' quelli con elementi circolari.
Concetto spaziale del 1957, rispondente alla tipologia dei 'muri', è caratterizzato da una forma centrale blu, né tonda, né a nucleo, costituita una porzione di tela ritagliata e incollata sulla superficie. In questo modo l'artista ottiene l'effetto voluto di un elemento sfuggente, sia per la particolare forma, sia per l'impercettibile consistenza volumetrica, che passa evidentemente in primo piano rispetto alla base grigia. Nel 1993 Jole De Sanna interpretava la serie dei 'gessi' in relazione a una mai sopita vena naturalistica: "Le terre, gli embrioni, i glutini arricchiscono il percorso di riferimenti naturali". La serie si raccorda, in realtà, alle tavolette in gesso colorate e graffite del 1931, da cui deriva il generale effetto a intonaco e gessoso. Dal 1954, quando le espone alla Biennale di Venezia riconnettendole alle ultime esperienze spazialiste, l'attenzione di Fontana nei confronti di quelle prime attestazioni di Astrattismo – anche nel vero e proprio rifacimento di alcuni esemplari distrutti dal tempo – intende cogliere l'essenza e trasfonderla in una nuova dimensione. In particolare, in questo esempio rimane dell'esperienza degli anni trenta una vaga suggestione, mentre si affaccia una sensibilità nuova: l'effetto di sospensione della forma nello spazio, il lirismo appena accennato delle sequenze di fori contribuiscono al significato di apparizione di una forma. Lo studio di elemento semplice, elementare, ma insieme ambiguo e sfuggente nelle sue dimensioni, a rilievo rispetto al fondo, pone Fontana in grande anticipo sulle riflessioni americane intorno alle 'strutture primarie'.

[1] J. De Sanna, *Lucio Fontana, materia, spazio, concetto*, Mursia, 1993, p 113.

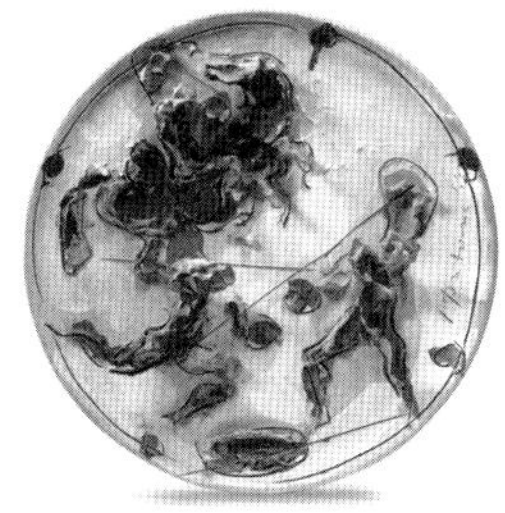

GUERRIERI, 1957

Terracotta colorata azzurro, rosa e nero
Diametro 47 cm

Firma e data incisi lungo il bordo: *l. fontana 57*

Provenienza
Milano, Galleria Marconi

Opera registrata presso l'Archivio della Fondazione Lucio Fontana, Milano con il numero 1900/257.

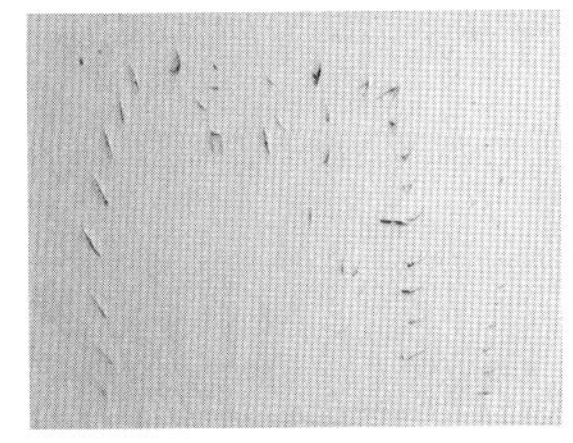

CONCETTO SPAZIALE, 1958

Tagli e strappi su carta telata, bianco
97 × 130 cm
Firma, titolo e data al retro: *l. fontana / Concetto spaziale / 1958*

Provenienza
Milano, collezione T.R.F.; Ginevra, collezione Nahmad

Esposizioni
1970 Torino, Galleria Civica d'Arte Moderna, *Lucio Fontana*, 5 febbraio - 28 marzo, n. 174, fig. 164;
2007 Londra, Estorick Collection of Modern Italian Art, *Lucio Fontana: At the Roots of Spatialism*, 27 giugno - 9 settembre;
2007 Milano-Londra, *Lucio Fontana, Sedici Sculture 1937-1967*, Amedeo Porro arte moderna e contemporanea, Ben Brown Fine Arts, Silvana Editoriale, Cinisello Balsamo, pp. 8-9;
2008 New York, Sperone Westwater, *ZERO* in *New York*, 6 novembre - 20 dicembre, p. 224;
2010 Londra, Ben Brown Fine Arts, *Heinz Mack / Lucio Fontana*, 6 ottobre - 21 dicembre, p. 45;
2012 Londra, Ben Brown Fine Arts e Amedeo Porro Arte Moderna e Contemporanea, *From De Chirico to Cattelan. A Survey of 20th Century Italian Art*, 8 ottobre - 30 novembre, p. 21.

Bibliografia
"Vernissage", *Kunst bis aufs messer: Lucio Fontana*, marzo 1960, n. 2;
E. Crispolti, *Lucio Fontana Catalogue Raisonné des peintures, sculptures et environnements spatiaux*, Edition La Connaissance, Bruxelles 1974, vol. II, pp. 76 e 77, n. 58 CA 2;
E. Crispolti, *Lucio Fontana, Catalogo Generale*, Edizioni Electa, Milano 1986, vol. I, p. 267, n. 58 CA 2;
E. Crispolti, *Lucio Fontana, Catalogo Ragionato di sculture, dipinti, ambientazioni*, Edizioni Skira, Milano 2006, vol. I, p. 434, n. 58 CA 2.

Il 16 febbraio 1957 Lucio Fontana, in seguito all'inaugurazione della mostra personale alla Galleria del Naviglio in cui aveva presentato soprattutto "pietre" e "barocchi", confidava all'amico Mario Bardini: "Come sempre dopo ogni mostra il periodo di crisi, lustrini o non lustrini?? Pittore o scultore?? Spaziale o realista? E così il tempo passa nella continua e beata illusione!". Nel suo universo creativo si preparava, ed egli ne era già consapevole in quel momento, il tempo della decantazione della propria pittura verso una dialettica di superficie e una più chiara formulazione tonale. Nel corso del 1958, d'altra parte, si intensificano i contatti con i giovani rappresentanti di una nuova sensibilità e in particolare con Piero Manzoni. Tra Fontana e Manzoni nasce e si consolida nel corso dell'anno una vera amicizia: l'artista più anziano promuove e assiste compiaciuto all'elaborazione dei primi "achrome" di Manzoni, di cui ammira quella nuova, chiara, oggettivazione della "tabula rasa". Forse suggestionato da questo nuovo clima milanese che nel corso del 1959 porterà alla ripubblicazione del testo di Guido Ballo per la sala di Fontana alla Biennale del 1958 con il titolo di *Oltre la pittura* sul primo numero di "Azimuth", l'artista perviene, verso la fine dell'anno, a una presa ulteriore di coscienza della necessità dell'azzeramento, uno dei principi fondanti la propria poetica. Fontana riparte dal nulla, dal foglio di carta e da un gesto ripetuto.

Il ciclo delle 'carte' conta in totale 50 opere documentate, e in particolare la serie rara di tre o quattro esemplari museali a cui appartiene *Concetto spaziale* del 1958 è la testimonianza di un nuovo inizio in cui la superficie della tela, irrigidita dalla carta incollata, viene a essere il "campo" di un'azione che ha una sua precisa grammatica segnica e un alto grado metaforico: il piccolo taglio, la fenditura si dispone a tracciare una sequenza ritmica. È come se l'artista provasse in questa breve serie di "carte" intelate il nuovo gesto del taglio, già sperimentato nel 1957 nei soffitti spaziali di Procchio e nel graffito murale Altimani a Milano, ma con un nuovo significato. Il taglio qui non è più associato ad alcun altro segno se non a se stesso e nella consequenzialità ripetuta genera una traccia, un movimento ondulatorio, rivela il processo stesso che l'ha generato. Il taglio non apre solo all'infinito, ma diviene metafora dell'azione stessa, ripetuta e irreversibile, dell'artista.

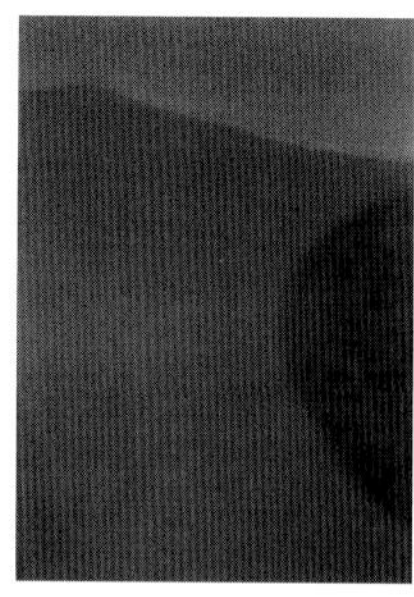

CONCETTO SPAZIALE, 1958

Anilina, matita, collage e buchi su tela, verde, azzurro, grigio chiaro e scuro
130 × 97 cm
Firma, titolo e data al retro: *L. Fontana/ Concetto Spaziale/1958*

Provenienza
Roma, Galleria Marlborough; Brescia, collezione Cattaneo; Monza, collezione privata; Milano, collezione privata; Amburgo, collezione privata.

Esposizioni
1963 L'Aquila, Castello Cinquecentesco, *Aspetti dell'arte contemporanea: omaggio a Cagli, omaggio a Fontana, omaggio a Quaroni – retrospettive archeologiche,* 28 luglio - 6 ottobre (*Omaggio a Fontana* testo e documentazione a cura di Enrico Crispolti), n. 140;
1966 Buenos Aires, Centro de Artes Visuales del Instituto Torcuato di Tella, *Lucio Fontana*, 26 luglio - 28 agosto, n. 16;
1966 Minneapolis, Walker Art Center; Austin, University of Texas Art Museum, *Lucio Fontana, The Spatial Concept of Art*, 6 gennaio - 13 febbraio, n. 18;
1967 Amsterdam, Stedelijk Museum, *Lucio Fontana - Concetti Spaziali*, 23 marzo - 7 maggio, n. 22; Eindhoven, Stedelijk van Abbemuseum, 12 maggio - 18 giugno, n. 22
1967 Humlebaek, Louisiana Museum, *Fontana*, gennaio-febbraio, n. 22;
1967 Stoccolma, Moderna Museet, *Fontana, Idéer om rymden*, 26 agosto - 1 ottobre, n. 22;
1968 Hannover, Kestner-Gesellschaft, *Lucio Fontana*, 25 gennaio - 25 febbraio, n. 22;
2002 Zurich, de Pury & Luxembourg, *Lucio Fontana*, 10 ottobre - 6 dicembre, n. 70;
2012 New York, Gagosian Gallery, *Lucio Fontana. Ambienti spaziali*, 3 maggio - 30 giugno, p. 239, n. 260; Londra, Ben Brown Fine Arts e Amedeo Porro Arte moderna e contemporanea, *From De Chirico to Cattelan. A Survey of 20th Century Italian*, 8 ottobre - 30 novembre, p. 25.

Bibliografia
E. Crispolti, *Omaggio a Fontana*, Beniamino Carucci Editore, Assisi-Roma 1971, p. 162, n. 170;
E. Crispolti, *Lucio Fontana Catalogue Raisonné des peintures, sculptures et environnements spatiaux*, Edition La Connaissance, Bruxelles 1974, vol. II, p. 63, n. 58 I 36;
E. Crispolti, *Lucio Fontana. Catalogo Generale*, Edizioni Electa, Milano 1986, vol. I, p. 218, n. 58 I 36;
E. Crispolti, *Lucio Fontana. Catalogo Ragionato di sculture, dipinti, ambientazioni*, Edizioni Skira, Milano 2006, vol. I, p. 377, n. 58 I 36.

"Quando si accorge di aver raggiunto il pieno dominio della materia, di aver sfruttato gli effetti più imprevisti e suggestivi, castiga la materia stessa, riduce ancora il suo linguaggio ai mezzi più essenziali [...] tutto, nelle recenti composizioni spaziali di Fontana, è ridotto ai mezzi più elementari, più semplici: si attua con estrema chiarezza nell'urgenza della voce, che è voce di artista inconfondibile." Con queste parole Guido Ballo presentava alla Biennale del 1958 il nuovo ciclo degli 'inchiostri', opere caratterizzate dall'uso delle aniline, spesso su tele montate al contrario in modo da sfruttare la parte grezza, e segnate da un immaginario fluttuante, che è stato definito anche 'nuagistico'.

In *Concetto spaziale* del 1958, il valore timbrico di pochi, essenziali toni genera un'atmosfera che non allude ad alcuna immagine, né a porzioni di oggetti, né a visioni sfuocate. Si tratta semplicemente di trasparenze che la leggerezza delle aniline lascia immaginare possano alludere a una porzione di paesaggio, senza però garantirne alcuna presenza. In posizione centrale galleggia un solo elemento, una piccola forma di tela ritagliata, segnata da due linee di impercettibili fori. La forma è emergente e a lieve rilievo rispetto al fondo, in un gioco ambiguo di spazi che sembrano trovare un'armonia naturale nella reciproca influenza e sovrapposizione. Il valore energetico e luminoso del colore, dominante in questa tela, non è compromesso dall'unica presenza che, al contrario, garantisce un breve lacerto di umanità e di esistenza, quasi l'ultima testimonianza

di una reazione umana alla perdita di ogni riferimento spazio-temporale.
Fin dai primi anni sessanta questo *Concetto spaziale* datato 1958 è considerato come una testimonianza emblematica di questa fase creativa dell'artista ed esposto nella prima importante mostra retrospettiva di Fontana curata da Enrico Crispolti al castello cinquecentesco dell'Aquila nel 1963.

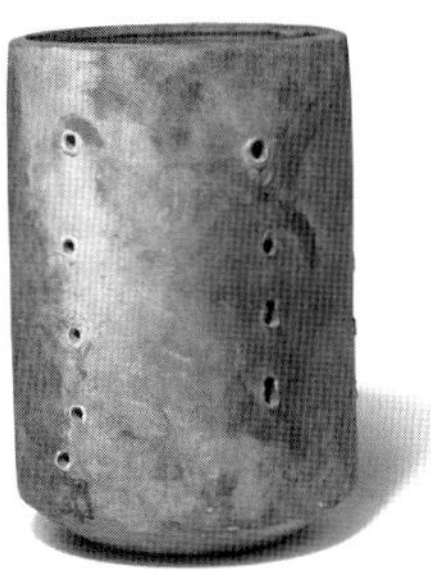

CONCETTO SPAZIALE, 1958

Terracotta con buchi dipinta a freddo
25 × 17,2 × 17,2 cm
Firma e data incise lungo la parte inferiore:
l. Fontana 58

Provenienza
Acquisito direttamente dall'artista dalla famiglia dell'attuale proprietario

Opera registrata presso l'Archivio della Fondazione Lucio Fontana, Milano con il numero 1737/104.

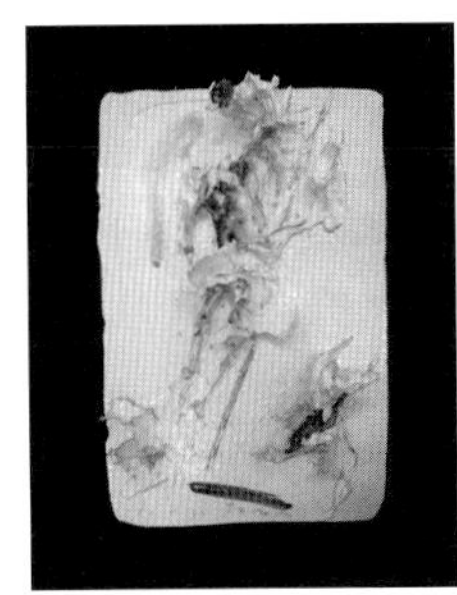

DEPOSIZIONE DALLA CROCE, 1959-1960

Ceramica riflessata, bianca e azzurra
53 × 35 cm
Firma incisa in basso: *l. fontana*

Provenienza
Milano, collezione Cattaneo

Opera registrata presso l'Archivio della Fondazione Lucio Fontana, Milano con il numero 386/2.

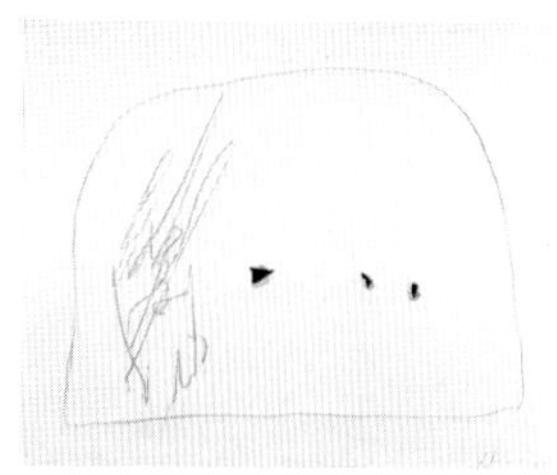

CONCETTO SPAZIALE, 1961

Olio, graffiti e buchi su tela, bianco
81 × 100 cm
Firma incisa in basso a destra: *l. Fontana*

Provenienza
Düsseldorf, Galerie Schmela; Düsseldorf, Galerie Gunar; Milano, collezione privata

Esposizioni
1961 Milano, Galleria Civica d'Arte Moderna e Roma, Palazzo delle Esposizioni, *Mostra della Critica Italiana 1961*, 13 febbraio - 11 marzo, p. 40, n. 44;
1969 Wuppertal, Kunst und Museumsverein, *Hommage à Fontana*, 20 settembre - 2 novembre, n. 25;
2010 Londra, Ben Brown Fine Arts, *Heinz Mack / Lucio Fontana*, 6 ottobre - 21 dicembre, pp. 48-51;
2012 Londra, Ben Brown Fine Arts e Amedeo Porro Arte moderna e contemporanea, *From De Chirico to Cattelan. A Survey of 20th Century Italian Art*, 8 ottobre - 30 novembre, p. 22.

Bibliografia
E. Crispolti, *Lucio Fontana. Catalogue Raisonné des peintures, sculptures et environnements spatiaux* , Edition La Connaissance, Bruxelles 1974, vol. II, p. 112, n. 61 O 65;
E. Crispolti, *Lucio Fontana, Catalogo Generale,* Edizioni Electa, Milano 1986, vol. I, p. 376, n. 61 O 65;
AA.VV. *Arte all'incanto*, Edizioni Longanesi & Co., Milano 1987, p. 240.
E. Crispolti, *Lucio Fontana, Catalogo Ragionato di sculture, dipinti, ambientazioni*, Edizioni Skira, Milano 2006, vol. II, p. 564, n. 61 O 65.

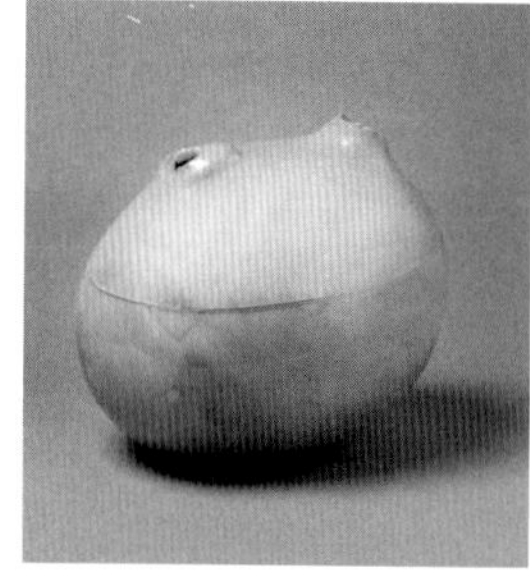

CONCETTO SPAZIALE, 1962-1964

Ceramica smaltata
27,8 × 22,5 × 23,5 cm
Firma incisa sotto la base: *L. Fontana*

Provenienza
New Hampshire, West Lebanon, Jan and Ingeborg van der Marck; Los Angels, Vidal Sassoon

Esposizioni
1963 Zurigo, Gimpel & Hanover, *Lucio Fontana peinture, sculpture*, 21 maggio - 15 giugno;
1966 Minneapolis, Minneapolis Walker Art Center, *Lucio Fontana. The Spatial Concept of Art*, 6 gennaio - 13 febbraio, n. 50, p. 13, poi Austin, University of Texas Art Museum;
1977 New York, The Solomon R. Guggenheim Museum, *Lucio Fontana 1899-1968: a retrospective*, 20 ottobre - 11 dicembre; *Retrospective*, 20 ottobre - 11 dicembre, n. 97, p. 101;
1986 New York, Marisa del Re Gallery, *Lucio Fontana Conquest of Space*, novembre-dicembre;
2007 Milano, Amedeo Porro arte moderna e contemporanea, *Lucio Fontana, Sedici Sculture*, 1937-1967, 12 dicembre - 28 febbraio, fig. 14, pp. 104-105 poi Londra Ben Brown Fine Arts, aprile-maggio;
2012 Londra, Ben Brown Fine Arts e Amedeo Porro Arte moderna e contemporanea, *From De Chirico to Cattelan. A Survey of 20th Century Italian Art*, 8 ottobre - 30 novembre, p. 26.

Bibliografia
P. Rouve, *Lucio Fontana*, in "Quadrum", Bruxelles 1963, n. 14, p. 53.

Opera registrata presso l'Archivio della Fondazione Lucio Fontana, Milano con il numero 3329/23.

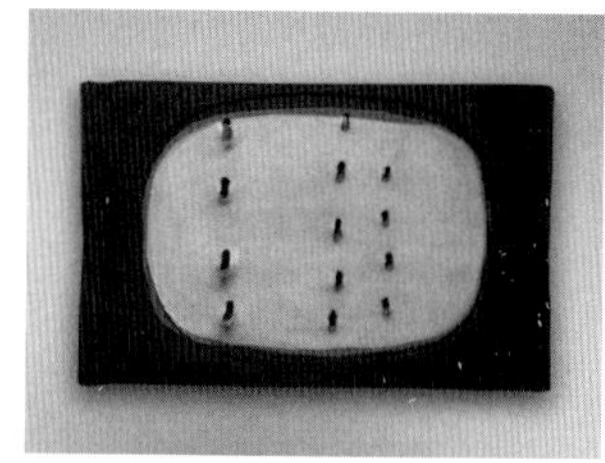

CONCETTO SPAZIALE, 1960-1965

Terracotta colorata
26, 5 × 41, 5 × 5 cm
Firma incisa in basso a destra: *l. Fontana*

Provenienza
Berna, Galleria Tony Gerber; Germania, collezione privata.

Esposizioni
2012 Londra, Ben Brown Fine Arts e Amedeo Porro Arte moderna e contemporanea, *From De Chirico to Cattelan. A Survey of 20th Century Italian Art*, 8 ottobre - 30 novembre, p. 19.

Opera registrata presso l'Archivio della Fondazione Lucio Fontana, Milano con il numero 2678/1.

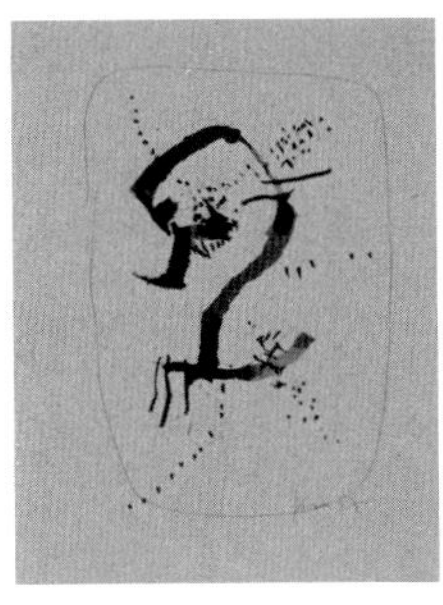

CONCETTO SPAZIALE, 1957

Inchiostri colorati su carta
25,9 × 20,2 cm
Firma e data in basso a destra: *fontana 57*

Provenienza
Dono dell'artista
Torino, Collezione Francesco de Bartolomeis; Torino, collezione privata.

Esposizioni
2005 Londra, Ben Brown Fine Arts, *Lucio Fontana. Paintings, Sculptures and Drawings*, 5 febbraio - 20 maggio, p. 75.

Bibliografia
L. M. Barbero, *Lucio Fontana. Catalogo Ragionato dei disegni e delle carte*, Edizioni Skira, Milano 2013, vol. I, p. 106; vol. III, p. 759, n. 57 DSP 50

Opera registrata presso l'Archivio della Fondazione Lucio Fontana, Milano con il numero 3329/16.

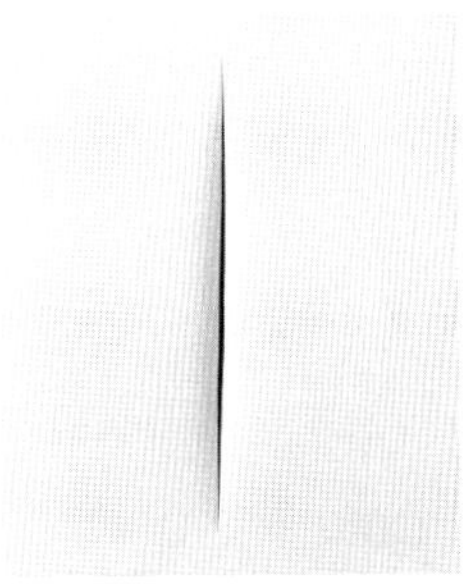

CONCETTO SPAZIALE. ATTESA, 1965

Idropittura su tela, bianco
54 × 45 cm
Firma, titolo, dedica e scritta sul retro:
l. Fontana / 'Concetto spaziale' /ATTESA / Tu [sic] Al Lerner / l. Fontana / il blu del cielo il / bleu del mare, il san- /gue blue

Provenienza
Milano, Studio Marconi; Valenza Po, collezione Franco Frascarolo; Piedmont, collezione privata; Londra, Ben Brown Fine Arts; Francia, collezione privata

Esposizioni
2000 Alessandria, ex Complesso Conventuale di San Francesco, *Lo sguardo indiscreto. Arte del XX Secolo dalle Collezioni Alessandrine*, 18 novembre - 14 gennaio 2001
2013 Valenza, Villa Scalcabarozzi, *Tesori d'Arte a Valenza. Capolavori dalle Collezioni Private*, 8 dicembre - 5 gennaio 2014, pp. 122-123

Bibliografia
E. Crispolti, *Lucio Fontana Catalogue Raisonné des peintures, sculptures et environnements spatiaux*, Edition La Connaissance, Bruxelles 1974, vol. II, p. 164, n. 65 T 86
E. Crispolti, *Lucio Fontana. Catalogo Generale*, Edizioni Electa, Milano 1986, vol. II, p. 576, n. 65 T 86
E. Crispolti, *Lucio Fontana. Catalogo Ragionato di sculture, dipinti, ambientazioni*, Edizioni Skira, Milano 2006, vol. II, p. 762, n. 65 T 86

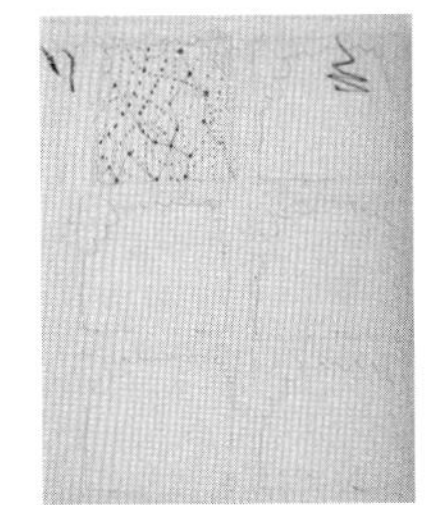
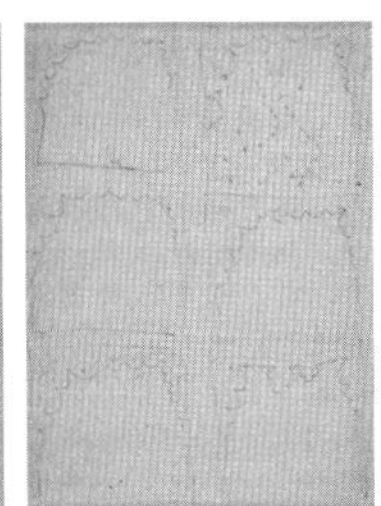

SEI STUDI PER TEATRINI, 1964-1966

Biro su carta
28 × 22 cm
recto e verso

Provenienza
Milano, collezione privata

Esposizioni
2012 Londra, Ben Brown Fine Arts e Amedeo Porro Arte moderna e contemporanea, *From De Chirico to Cattelan. A Survey of 20th Century Italian Art*, 8 ottobre - 30 novembre, p. 20.

Bibliografia
L. M. Barbero, *Lucio Fontana. Catalogo Ragionato dei disegni e delle carte*, Edizioni Skira, Milano 2013, vol. III, p. 939, n. 64-65 DSP 310

Opera registrata presso l'Archivio della Fondazione Lucio Fontana, Milano con il numero 1900/205

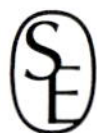

Silvana Editoriale

Direction
Dario Cimorelli

Art Director
Giacomo Merli

Editing
Lorena Ansani

Translations
InEdita, Milano

Layout
Mirco Ameglio

Production Coordinator
Michela Bramati

Editorial Assistant
Ondina Granato

Photo Editor
Alessandra Olivari, Silvia Sala

Press Office
Lidia Masolini, press@silvanaeditoriale.it

Silvana Editoriale S.p.A.
via Margherita De Vizzi, 86
20092 Cinisello Balsamo, Milano
tel. 02 61 83 63 37
fax 02 61 72 464
www.silvanaeditoriale.it

Reproductions,
printing and binding in Italy
Printed
March 2015

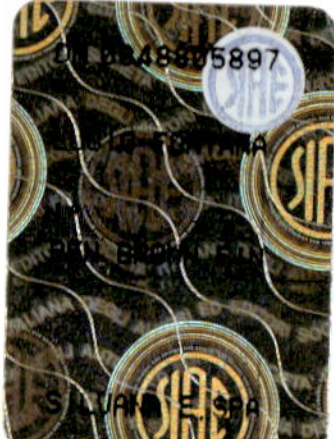